Praise for *The Innovation Blind Spot*

"We know a lot about what it takes to generate new ideas—but so little about how to recognize the ones that are worth pursuing. *The Innovation Blind Spot* is here to change that. It's a terrific read, with vivid data and memorable examples to help you stop betting on flops and spot the hits hiding right under your nose."

—Adam Grant, *New York Times* **bestselling author of** *Originals* **and** *Give and Take*

"Every entrepreneur with a great idea should have a fundamental right to start a business. But today, far too many barriers in society prevent the best people from competing. In this book, Ross outlines compelling strategies to find the best innovations—no matter where they are."

—Wendy Guillies, president and CEO, Ewing Marion Kauffman Foundation

"In this time of seismic shifts, our businesses, our governments, and our communities need to work together for our society to succeed—and we need new ideas to get there. Baird identifies the outliers that no one's betting on, and compellingly outlines how we can bring them into the mainstream."

—Governor Deval L. Patrick, managing director, Bain Capital Double Impact

"Every single city and community has the power to change the world. But to realize that power, we have to find the ideas and entrepreneurs that people aren't paying attention to. In *The Innovation Blind Spot*, Ross shows us how to do just that."

—Brad Feld, cofounder, Foundry Group; author of *Startup Communities*; **and coauthor of** *Venture Deals* **and** *Startup Opportunities*

"There's a myth that the innovation economy is a meritocracy, but unfortunately your background and your network still play a huge role in success. Ross makes a compelling case for how we can access the untapped potential in our innovation economy."

—Donna Byrd, founding publisher of *The Root* and vice president of Digital Media at Univision Communications

THE
INNOVATION
BLIND SPOT

THE
INNOVATION
BLIND SPOT

WHY WE BACK THE WRONG IDEAS—
AND WHAT TO DO ABOUT IT

ROSS BAIRD

BenBella Books, Inc.
Dallas, TX

BenBella

BenBella Books, Inc.
10440 N. Central Expressway, Suite 800
Dallas, TX 75231
www.benbellabooks.com
Send feedback to feedback@benbellabooks.com

Printed in the United States of America
10 9 8 7 6 5 4 3 2 1

Library of Congress Cataloging-in-Publication Data
Names: Baird, Ross, 1984- author.
Title: The innovation blind spot : why we back the wrong ideas—and what
   to do about it / Ross Baird.
Description: Dallas, TX : BenBella Books, Inc., [2017] | Includes
   bibliographical references and index.
Identifiers: LCCN 2017011827 (print) | LCCN 2017029235 (ebook) | ISBN
   9781944648626 (electronic) | ISBN 9781944648619 (trade cloth : alk. paper)
Subjects: LCSH: Technological innovations—Economic aspects—United States. |
   Entrepreneurship—United States. | Economic development—United states.
Classification: LCC HC110.T4 (ebook) | LCC HC110.T4 B25 2017 (print) | DDC
   338/.0640973—dc23
LC record available at https://lccn.loc.gov/2017011827

Editing by Laurel Leigh
Copyediting by Karen Wise
Proofreading by Chris Gage and Sarah Vostok
Indexing by Jigsaw Indexing Services
Text design by Publishers' Design
   and Production Services, Inc.

Text composition by PerfecType,
   Nashville, TN
Cover design by Kit Sweeney
Jacket design by Ivy Koval
Printed by Lake Book
   Manufacturing

Distributed by Perseus Distribution
www.perseusdistribution.com

To place orders through Perseus Distribution:
Tel: (800) 343-4499
Fax: (800) 351-5073
E-mail: orderentry@perseusbooks.com

For Jen

CONTENTS

FOREWORD

In 2013, I met Jen Medbery, the founder and CEO of a young edtech company called Kickboard. Jen was a software developer who had also spent three years as a middle school math teacher. She developed a tool that analyzed reliable data on each student to provide teachers with actionable insight. Today, Kickboard serves more than two hundred schools in twenty states. One might assume that Kickboard's growth was nurtured by a Silicon Valley accelerator, spurred by Sand Hill Road venture capitalist dollars, and built by Stanford engineers. In fact, Kickboard was started in the heart of New Orleans.

And Kickboard is not alone. The destruction that Hurricane Katrina brought about led to a citywide surge in charter schools, bringing passionate teachers, administrators, and education reformers together and paving the way for a burgeoning edtech industry in the city. New Orleans took a crisis and turned it into an opportunity. Pre-Katrina, only 30 percent of schools had a passing grade. The reinvention of the New Orleans school system has led to a reimagination of how teachers should teach and how students can learn, and the city has become a hotbed of startup innovation.

Jen is one of thousands of entrepreneurs I've met as I've criss-crossed the country over the past several years, first as chair of the Startup America Partnership and then as I've toured the country on Rise of the Rest bus tours organized by my investment firm, Revolution. We've traveled six thousand miles and visited twenty-six cities so far. It has been eye-opening to see how many cities are spawning startup cultures and incubating great startups. Meeting so many entrepreneurs in so many places has inspired me to redouble my efforts to do what I can to be sure that everybody everywhere has a shot at the American Dream.

It's not just about creating companies. It's also about creating the jobs that will propel the communities in which they operate. And these entrepreneurs—in what some call "flyover country"— are spawning breakthrough companies in sectors that matter most to us. The local expertise available in Rise of the Rest cities bodes well for the revolution that is accelerating in big industries such as healthcare, agriculture, and financial services.

Ross Baird shares a commitment to supporting entrepreneurs in unexpected places. Ross, and the firm he founded, Village Capital, have helped us shine a spotlight on great founders building impressive businesses throughout the country. Ross has joined us on each of our Rise of the Rest bus tours—and it was Ross who introduced me to Jen and Kickboard.

Ross has been a pioneer when it comes to blending profit and purpose. Historically, "what's good for business" and "what's good for society" have fallen into, as Ross likes to put it, two different pockets, but Village Capital actively invests in the sectors most ripe for disruption. These impact-focused "startup" companies have the potential to change the way billions of people live every day.

I first met Ross in 2014 when we served on a national commission convened by the University of Virginia to answer the question "Can startups save the American Dream?" I was struck by his hands-on approach to empowering entrepreneurs—no matter their background or geography—from the bottom up. Today, I see an innovation economy that too often works top-down. The best-connected people in the most resource-rich places are awash in opportunity, but most aspiring entrepreneurs don't have a chance.

Investors everywhere have blind spots, and as a result, we're overlooking most great ideas. Three-quarters of venture capital goes to founders in just three states: New York, California, and Massachusetts. Some 10 percent goes to women founders, and just 1 percent to African Americans. That's not right—and it's not smart. We need everybody on the playing field if we're going to remain the most innovative, entrepreneurial nation in the world.

Ross's work has been intentionally focused on democratizing access for entrepreneurs from all backgrounds, and by changing the paradigm in terms of how investors invest. Village Capital empowers entrepreneurs themselves to make the investing decisions. It's a unique approach that I hope others emulate, as it can help unearth breakthrough ideas, and also help level the playing field.

We're living in turbulent times. The world is changing rapidly, and as we witnessed from the 2016 election results, many people feel like they are being left behind in our economy. And many people are. We need to find—and promote—entrepreneurs and innovators everywhere, not just those who went to the best schools, know the right people, and live in the most developed innovation cities. We need more founders from diverse backgrounds, more companies from places outside the hotbeds of Silicon Valley, New York, and Boston, and a better understanding of how to build companies that deliver a holistic view of value—to their shareholders, to customers, and to society.

In my 2015 book, *The Third Wave*, I highlighted some of these companies. We're going to need more entrepreneurs like Kristin Richmond, CEO of Revolution Foods, who is changing food systems by improving the nutritional quality of school lunches across America. And we'll need more companies like Shinola, which is rewriting Detroit's story by creating quality manufacturing jobs in the middle of a once-great community that is again on the rise. I hope these "profit plus purpose" companies soon join the pantheon of iconic American entrepreneurial success stories.

I have no doubt that the trends Ross writes about in this book will gain steam. I have faith that the rest will rise, and we'll see new cities yielding the next great group of entrepreneurs. I am confident that entrepreneurship will be more inclusive, and that the faces of famous entrepreneurs you'll see over the next couple of decades will look very different from the average venture capital firm's portfolio today. Most importantly, I know that as the Internet continues to integrate with our daily life, startups will matter more to the things we do every day—how we eat, how we learn, how we live—than ever before. We saw tremendous innovation in the Internet's first and second waves, but we've still just scratched the surface in terms of what's possible.

What remains to be seen is what communities, what firms, what investors, and what countries will benefit from these changes. The jury is out, because it all depends on what happens next. The people who embrace these changes will have better economies and more thriving societies; the people who stick to old patterns will fall behind.

If you want to be a part of the success of the next wave of entre-preneurship, read on. In *The Innovation Blind Spot*, Ross shares a unique and invaluable viewpoint on what's broken in the innova-tion economy—and offers a compelling playbook for how to fix it. He will inspire you with stories of groundbreaking entrepreneurs, share unique and unexpected approaches to bringing more people into the entrepreneurial world, and, most importantly, help you identify your own blind spots so that collectively, we can make sure that every entrepreneur with a great idea, no matter who they are or where they live, really does have a shot at the American Dream.

—Steve Case

INTRODUCTION

I'm going to assume two things about you.

First, I'll assume that you're someone who is trying to do the right thing every day and wants to play a part in making the world a better place.

Second, I'll assume that you believe that capitalism, and the free markets and individual liberties it represents, is the best way for our global society to function. Even if you're critical of parts of the capitalist system today, you still believe, to borrow Winston Churchill's line about democracy, that it's "the worst system, except for all the others that have been tried."

But huge parts of the system aren't working. New firm creation in the United States is at a thirty-year low. The biggest investment firms in the country's wealthiest cities aren't delivering the best financial returns. And the structural problems in the system make all our other problems nearly impossible to solve. Even though we have more computing power in our pockets today than the entire world did fifty years ago, our food systems struggle to feed the world's growing population, and our health and education infrastructure can't take care of the current generation, let alone prepare the next one to lead.

We look to "innovation," which I'm going to define as new ideas, to help figure out solutions to these problems. When I say innovation, your mind might jump to Silicon Valley–style technology—and we'll spend a lot of time on that topic in this book. But innovation can be anything: a better way for your company to work, a new idea that can help your community, an amazing song or piece of art you create.

While a daily skim of *Forbes* or *Fortune* might make it seem as though we live in a golden age of innovation, most entrepreneurs today don't see it that way. In this book, I'll argue that most great innovations don't see the light of day, for reasons entirely of our own making.

The idea that entrepreneurship is a meritocracy is a myth. In the real world, money flows to the ideas that are the most convenient to find or the most familiar, not necessarily those that are the best. Simply put, the blind spots in the way we innovate—the way we nurture, support, and invest in new ideas—make all our other problems even harder to solve.

THE BLIND SPOTS IN OUR INNOVATION PROCESS

I've always been an entrepreneur, pursuing and building new ideas. I formally joined this conversation in 2009, when I founded a venture capital firm, Village Capital. I'm going to explore innovation from the vantage point of venture capital, because it is a helpful proxy for how we pick which big ideas we value as a society.

"Venture capital" is the most visible way that we invest in future ideas. "Venture capital funds" often have billions of dollars under management, and the very smart people who run these funds are in a position to pick "the next big idea," knowing that many will fail but some will win big. This structure largely dictates how our economy picks which ideas will drive the next generation. Entrepreneurs, funded by venture capitalists, launched five of the six most valuable companies in the world (Apple, Google, Microsoft, Facebook, Amazon). (The sixth company, Berkshire Hathaway, is a very large investment firm.)

You can innovate in other ways—for example, in philanthropy, inside your own company, or in government. As we'll discuss, these areas have their own issues, but perhaps most relevant to you is that they all share many of the same blind spots that exist within the venture capital industry.

As you'll see, innovation today suffers from three major blind spots. The first has to do with *how* we pick new ideas, the second with *where* we find new ideas and *who* we invest in, and the third with *why*—why we invest in new ideas to begin with. Each blind spot opens onto the next, like a set of nesting dolls. And they cause us to miss out on massive untapped potential in innovation: untapped companies, untapped markets, and entire untapped industries.

Let's start with the first blind spot, which centers on process: *how* we invest.

1. *"One size fits all."*

There's an ancient Greek myth of a demigod, Procrustes, who had a large house on the main road outside Athens. Hospitality was perhaps the most important value in ancient Greece (the Trojan War was launched on account of an ungracious host), and Procrustes was legendary for hosting guests and providing a bed that fit each guest perfectly. But he had a morbid secret: he would cut off the limbs of the guests who were too tall, and he would stretch the limbs of the guests who were too short.

We need to make decisions all the time, but the average human brain can only remember three or four things simultaneously. Facing an onslaught of information, we often use shortcuts, like "one size fits all" structures, to make the best decisions we can. In this book, we'll look at the rules and patterns we use to make decisions. These rules can sometimes be helpful. Too often, though, they limit our ability to innovate. As author and economist Nassim

Nicholas Taleb points out, we don't notice how we are constraining ourselves and our investments by applying one principle to all of them: "We seem unaware of this backward fitting, much like tailors who take great pride in delivering the perfectly fitting suit—but do so by surgically altering the limbs of their customers."[1]

In this book, I'll outline how the "one size fits all" structure currently being used to discover and support new innovations, most easily identified with venture capital, isn't necessarily the best structure for most ideas. In fact, a core piece of how we invest is a holdover from the nineteenth century whaling industry, and its universal applicability has rarely been challenged. The result: the "venture capital" way of decision-making doesn't always find the best ideas, regardless of whether they look like a New England whale or a Silicon Valley unicorn.

2. "It's not what you know; it's who you know."

The second blind spot happens interpersonally, and has to do with *where* our society's investments go. This starts with *who* we invest in.

We tend to look for innovation by investing in the people, places, and industries we know—the people who look like us, and are in our same tribe because of where they grew up or the schools they attended. In 2015, 78 percent of startup investment in the United States—and half of all startup investment in the world—went to three states: Massachusetts, New York, and California. Less than 5 percent of investments in the United States went to female founders, and less than 1 percent went to companies started by African-Americans and Latinos. From 2007 to 2012, 10 percent of all startup financing in the world went to graduates of just six universities (Stanford, Harvard, Berkeley, MIT, NYU, and UPenn).[2]

Free-market economists would maintain that New York City and San Francisco get more money because they're more productive than other places. But in reality, "It's not what you know; it's who you know" drives resource allocation. As I'll discuss later on, people pick ideas from people close to them and similar to them, rather than what might be the best idea. Most great ideas never even get on investors' radar.

3. "Two-pocket thinking."

The third blind spot has to do with *why* we invest, and the self-defeating barriers we put up between what we do and what we value.

I once pitched a successful businesswoman and philanthropist—let's call her Jane—on investing in an education technology company. This business was growing rapidly in revenue while at the same time improving student outcomes in low-income schools. Jane said, "Ross, I have two pockets. In my business pocket, I make as much money as I can. Once I have enough to provide for my family, I give generously from my philanthropy pocket. Which pocket are you asking about here?"

The blind spot: we artificially separate our jobs and our careers from our values. In this book, I'll argue that when we integrate *what* we do with *why* we do it, we get better results. As one example: In 2015 and 2016, Wharton and Cambridge Associates released separate studies that illustrated how when investors integrate financial returns with a broader social or environmental purpose, the financial returns were as good as—or, in some cases, better than—those of traditional investment firms.

The innovation economy hasn't learned this lesson. We too often invest in the ideas we think we can flip quickly, rather than the most important ones. Silicon Valley startups, almost to the point of parody, often talk about how they are "changing the world." Often, however, they disappoint. For example, in November 2016, the Silicon Valley startup June debuted a $1,500 countertop oven—after raising $30 million in venture capital. The

toaster didn't work. "Automated yet distracting. Boastful yet medi-
ocre. Confident yet wrong," read *Fast Company* journalist Mark
Wilson's review, highlighting the toaster as "everything that's
wrong with Silicon Valley."[3]

By focusing on $1,500 toasters, the innovation economy is giv-
ing short shrift to entire untapped industries—from healthcare to
education to energy. But as I'll show in the second section, a growing movement of "illuminators" are lighting up our blind spots.

HOW WE INVEST MATTERS JUST AS MUCH AS WHAT WE INVEST IN

The venture mind-set—a desire to bet on big ideas and to create
solutions to problems you see, even if it involves some personal
risk—is a worthy one. Venture capital has given us transformative
companies such as Apple and Google. Many of these companies
allow you to improve your life: you can get a fair interest-rate loan
if you've been using payday lenders (LendUp), buy more affordable
eyeglasses (Warby Parker), and make your home more energy-
efficient (Nest). And venture philanthropy—applying the venture
capital mind-set to nonprofits—has given us leading social innovations in microfinance and education reform.

But venture capital's blind spots are causing us to miss out
on too many innovative ideas—and this isn't good for anybody.
When, in January 2016, I reviewed the industries of over 150 "unicorn" companies, I found that only 15 percent of the enterprises
were solving problems in the top six areas that the majority of
the world's population spends its budget on: food, health, energy,
agriculture, financial services, and housing.

I wrote this book because I'm worried, and I'm baffled. I'm
worried that only 15 percent of our billion-dollar innovations are
solving the biggest problems people face in the real world, and that
the resources we're putting into new ideas are concentrated among

so few people in so few places. As we'll see in the first chapter, our blind spots are causing the death of what we know as the American Dream and preventing many other great ideas around the world from having a chance to begin with. And I'm baffled that the American Dream seems to have been confused with the Silicon Valley Dream, which means that more people don't see these opportunities outside the mainstream.

This book comes from the perspective of someone who is inside the system: I'm a white guy who was born in the United States, went to good schools, and was lucky to have a family who had the time and resources to support me. I have had a lot of built-in advantages in the free market. While I've worked hard and am proud of my success, I am aware and grateful that I've never had a shortage of opportunities.

But having participated in this system as an investor and an entrepreneur, I see that the status quo doesn't always allocate resources to the best and the brightest. Instead, the ones who are closest to capital, and know the right people, go to the front of the line. In the coming chapters, I'll identify when and why this happens—and who is making progress solving the problem.

This book will first explain the blind spots that cause the dysfunction in our innovation system; second, highlight an emerging group of people who are thinking about how to illuminate these blind spots; and third, outline some steps you can take in your own life to become aware of these blind spots and make a difference. Finally, I'll explore what it means to build an ecosystem—and what all this means for the American Dream.

We're at an inflection point in our society. The people who make decisions over which problems we're going to solve are often disconnected from the problems that matter the most. Instead of solving the biggest problems of the day, we're putting billions of dollars into how to make mobile advertising and clickbait news more effective, and nudging people to buy more stuff.

But there's reason for optimism. If we're aware of our blind spots, we can break bad habits and create new ways of investing. And there are already people building a movement of how to innovate better. This movement revolutionizes entrepreneurship—but more broadly, any innovation—by giving anyone with a great idea a better chance.

This movement will actually change the world. Join me in the journey.

PART I

THE INNOVATION
BLIND SPOT

CHAPTER 1

WHAT HAPPENED TO THE
AMERICAN DREAM?

To me, the American Dream is being able to follow your
own personal calling. To be able to do what you want to do
is incredible freedom.
  —Maya Lin

I have spent my life judging the distance between American
reality and the American dream.
  —Bruce Springsteen

The 2016 United States presidential election revealed a massive
blind spot in our society—and caught most people completely
by surprise.

Fortune 500 leaders in Armani suits and Hermès ties, tech
CEOs in company T-shirts, academics, and the political and media
elite coalesced, nearly unanimously, around Hillary Clinton's
candidacy. Virtually every poll and computer forecast predicted
Secretary Clinton's victory. When Donald Trump won the majority
of states and the presidency, the public dialogue in many parts of
the country revolved around one question: "How could we have
missed this?"

The election illustrates one basic truth that no poll can capture in full: many people feel that the basic social contract of the
American Dream—if you have a great idea, solve problems, and
work hard, you'll be successful—is not true in an ever-globalizing
world. This contract is not working for them. While no single

3

lens can ever capture the commotion of a country as large, or an economy as dynamic, as the United States, entrepreneurship is a particularly useful lens, and one that I hope will resonate with many readers—even those who are not in the business of building, funding, or supporting startups.

Entrepreneurship represents the American Dream distilled: anyone with a vision—for their business, their family, their community, their country—should have a fair shot at success, on the merits of that vision and that vision alone. I'll explore how we're living up to that standard through stories of entrepreneurs you know, and also stories of those you may not know yet.

ENTREPRENEURSHIP IN CRISIS

As AOL cofounder Steve Case likes to say, America itself was once a startup—250 years ago. Throughout American history, entrepreneurs from Ben Franklin to Mark Zuckerberg have made the country a world leader through their tremendous visions.

Entrepreneurs also build the future of our economy. Our economy's dynamic nature has always depended on what economist Joseph Schumpeter called "creative destruction." Firms that fail to provide value die; better ideas take their place. A 2015 report by the Kauffman Foundation showed that nearly 100 percent of net new jobs in America are created by firms that are less than five years old.[4] In the long run, startups create all our new jobs.

But there's a problem: entrepreneurship is in crisis. In most places in the United States, entrepreneurs aren't succeeding.

It has never been better to be a big company in America; in 2016 there were more big companies than at any time in the last century. But it has rarely been a worse time to be an entrepreneur. Although a new business starts every two minutes, another firm closes its doors every eighty seconds—the highest rate of firm death in the past fifty years.[5] In 1980, nearly half of American firms were five years old or younger. By 2015, that number had fallen to one-third.[6] According to the nonpartisan Economic Innovation Group, fewer Americans are starting successful firms than at any point in the last century.[7]

And the innovation in our economy isn't very evenly dispersed. In the past, America's innovation economy was remarkably dynamic, according to the Economic Innovation Group. In the thirty years prior to the Great Recession of 2008, in 80 percent of the US's 366 metro areas, more firms started than died, on average, every year. But the dynamism of the US economy is highly concentrated today: in 2014, only 33 percent of metro areas saw more firms born than die.

FIRM BIRTH (STARTUP) AND DEATH RATES

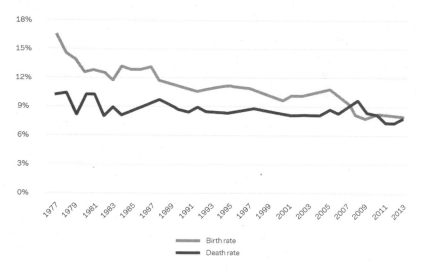

Source: Economic Innovation Group[8]

METRO AREAS WITH INCREASING (LEFT) AND DECREASING (RIGHT) NUMBERS OF FIRMS IN 2014

142 metro areas saw a **rise** in firms in 2014   **224** metro areas saw a **decline** in firms in 2014

Source: Census BDS

Source: Economic Innovation Group[9]

This might come as a surprise. On its face, it might appear that more entrepreneurs are realizing the American Dream than ever before. Over the last decade, entrepreneurs have launched over 150 companies that became "unicorns"—what the media has come to call VC-backed companies worth more than $1 billion. Thanks to these unicorns, you can order a box of treats for your dog, purchase a ready-to-cook evening meal, book your next airline flight, and manage your fantasy sports league—all without leaving your home. The faces of their founders smile at you from airport bookstores, so familiar that they inspire parody on TV and in movies.

But the definition of a blind spot is something we don't know that we're missing. And our investing culture's blind spots are causing us to ignore places, people, and ideas in a way that stifles innovation and make it difficult for most entrepreneurs to realize the American Dream.

WHY OUR INNOVATION BLIND SPOTS ARE DESTROYING THE AMERICAN DREAM

In 1991, the Haitian army had just deposed President Jean-Bertrand Aristide, and the country was on the brink of civil war. Ten-year-old Jerry Nemorin and his family escaped the chaos and resettled in Florida.

Jerry's first experience with the US financial system was when his mom tried to buy a car. Twenty-five years later, Jerry still remembers the sign above the auto lot: "BUY HERE, PAY HERE." Jerry's mom was an immigrant and didn't have any credit, so she took out a loan directly from the shop. "I was only twelve," remembers Jerry, "but looking through the loan documents, I saw that the interest on the loan would cost more than the car itself." But Jerry's mom didn't have a choice.

Jerry attended the University of Florida and then got a job on Wall Street. He saw more and more Americans experiencing the same financial problems that his mom had. Banks had enormous incentive to finance and then refinance consumers, and consumers were getting into more and more trouble with credit. "Predatory firms were taking advantage of the moment," Jerry said.

In 2008 the Great Recession hit the country like a storm. Amid the financial wreckage, Jerry, who had left his Wall Street job for business school at the University of Virginia, had an idea. He knew that 50 percent of Americans do not have enough savings to deal with a $400 emergency.[10] But he also knew—from experience—that many consumers are responsible with their money; they just get into a series of unlucky situations, like a large medical debt, that can ruin their credit for life. If Jerry could buy up the collected debt of hundreds, thousands, even millions of consumers, he could work with them to restructure their debt and reclaim their financial health—that is, help them rather than prey on them.

Jerry founded LendStreet shortly after the recession. He hired a small team and started operations. After a few months, Jerry was building the business steadily, but he needed more money to grow. At first, he wasn't successful—and he had a hunch why. Investors like to follow patterns; they often use the phrase "pattern recognition" to justify decisions regarding where to invest their money. And when it came to patterns, Jerry had three big problems.

First, as an African-American, Jerry doesn't look like most people who are successful raising money. In 2015, less than 1 percent of venture capital went to African-Americans and Latinos (and only 7 percent went to white women).[11]

Second, as an immigrant, Jerry's family did not have long-standing connections, and the innovation economy is highly relationship-driven.

Finally, as a founder building a company around debt solutions for people without a lot of money, Jerry was solving a hard problem that didn't resonate with the average venture capitalist. The mission of LendStreet, to get Americans out of deep debt, might have touched their hearts, but it never reached their wallets.

Venture capitalists, Jerry says, "want to solve my-world problems, but forget about real-world problems. Silicon Valley has become a place where you try and solve the problem of convenience. I find that people are dismissive of ideas that they don't empathize with. It's much harder to make decisions, and take the time, to diligence a problem you've never faced, but it is the most important thing you can do."

Jerry simply didn't fit anyone's pattern. As he puts it, "When it comes to pattern recognition, living far away from VC funds in central Virginia, as a black guy, solving a problem for poor people, I was 0 for 3!"[12]

In 2014, the firm I founded, Village Capital, was able to connect Jerry to a network of partners and potential funders. Soon after, he got a boost from Silicon Valley firm Kapor Capital, which intentionally invests in underrepresented founders. He picked up his life from central Virginia, where he had friends, family, and a community, and moved to Cupertino, California, right near Apple headquarters. In mid-2016, LendStreet raised nearly $40 million from private lenders to help hundreds of Americans break free of debt.

Jerry's idea—helping consumers get out of debt—has been both successful and incredibly effective. He was able to break into the system and succeed, and as a result, he's already helped over a thousand customers. Here's a typical example: One of Jerry's customers, let's call him Daniel, came to LendStreet in crisis. He had been married for nearly two years when his wife was diagnosed with cancer. Collectively, they had amassed $58,000 in student and medical debt. Through LendStreet, Daniel was able to refinance his home, consolidate his debts, and raise his credit score from 625 to 808. Within a year, he had cut his debt to $33,000, and with a healthy credit score he was well on his way to financial health.

Thanks to a few strokes of good luck and good timing, Jerry was able to fit into the rigid requirements of venture capital. When he needed to move to the Bay Area, he was young, single, and flexible and could thus pick up at a moment's notice. But what if he hadn't been introduced to investors who could back him? What if he couldn't, or didn't want to, leave his hometown for Silicon Valley? What if, like so many Americans, he could not afford to move to one of the wealthiest zip codes in the country?

The simple truth: the current model for venture capital—for backing new ideas—is bad for all founders who don't fit the pattern. It's bad for investors, too, because the biggest venture capital firms, concentrated in the biggest cities, aren't necessarily set up to invest in the most innovative ideas. And the current model is bad for the American Dream, because there are so many people like Jerry—people who have a great idea but don't fit the expected pattern. That in turn can destroy the cohesiveness and social fabric of our society, especially as the reality of the system starts to sink in.

The way we invest is only worsening already-deep divides: the states that voted for Donald Trump in the 2016 presidential election received only 15 percent of all venture capital in 2015.[13] But this disaffection goes far deeper than one election. The decline of the American entrepreneurial economy affects anyone—Republicans and Democrats; African-Americans, Latinos, and Caucasians; women and men—who lives in the blind spots. In order to truly live up to its promise of being able to change the world, entrepreneurship needs to be accessible to everyone.

One of my inspirations for writing this book was *New Yorker* staff writer George Packer's best seller *The Unwinding.* Packer describes how the last forty years have seen an unraveling of the very fabric of the American Dream, and how we've reached a point at which the political and social structure is unsustainable. As Packer points out, celebrities and successful businesspeople have never had it better, but most people have lost both community and economic security, and, ultimately, meaning in their lives.

Entrepreneurs and innovators creating new jobs are perhaps the most critical part of the path out of America's morass. Packer is ultimately optimistic, and so am I. Yet if investors and entrepreneurs think that we can catalyze an economic revival by continuing with the same playbook we've used for decades, we're going to lose the game in a landslide.

CHAPTER 2

CHASING WHALES AND UNICORNS

*Why the Venture Capital Process Causes
Us to Miss Out on Most Ideas*

To accomplish his object, Ahab must use tools: and of all
tools used in the shadow of the moon, men are most apt to
get out of order.
　　　—Herman Melville, *Moby-Dick; or, The Whale*

Why do millions of entrepreneurs like Jerry Nemorin sit in
blind spots? In the introduction, we talked about what happens when we overlook great ideas. In the next few chapters, we'll talk about the many ways we overlook new ideas, leading us to miss out on untapped companies, markets, and industries that can be successful.

For most people, "innovation" means *what* we invest in: Where's the next Uber or Lyft? But there's been very little innovation in *how* we find ideas. As one tangible example, most of the venture capital process today is a "one size fits all" system that has its origins in nineteenth-century whaling.

A HISTORY OF THE CHASE: FROM THE WHITE WHALE TO THE UNICORN

Before the dawn of electricity, cities powered their streets and lit houses with the most efficient form of energy on hand: whale oil.

Long before the days of ExxonMobil, whaling was a wildly profitable industry; according to Harvard professors Tom Nicholas and Jonas Peter Akins, returns on investment for a whaling expedition regularly reached three times the return in agriculture.[14] Naturally, wealthy families sought to invest in whaling ships. But unlike putting up money for a new tavern or planting a crop, whaling was an expensive pastime. The typical voyage required an up-front investment of up to $30,000, nearly ten times the operating cost of the average manufacturing firm. Even families with money could rarely finance a voyage alone. And the voyages were risky: one in three lost money, and only a few netted huge returns.

People wanted to invest in whaling expeditions, but didn't know how. In the 1830s, a cottage industry was born out of this dilemma. A new class of independent "agents" began to pool money from multiple families, recruit a ship and a captain, and assume responsibility for the voyage. If the voyage succeeded, they would split the profits from the sale of the whale oil among the investors. With the help of agents, investors were now able to finance multiple voyages at once. As "limited partners," they weren't allowed to second-guess the captain's decisions. Their capital was spread across multiple voyages, so one very lucrative tour could offset the loss of another ship.[15] Today's limited partnerships in venture capital use much the same model, hardly changed from the 1800s. But it doesn't end there.

To finance the day-to-day operations of whaling voyages, the agents, investors, and ship captains developed a structure for who got paid what. At the end of a voyage, the crew would return to port with their whale fat, known as their "carry." The crew would get 20 percent of the carry, with investors retaining the other 80 percent. (*Moby-Dick* describes a spirited argument in which the crew negotiates about the "lay" they get after the voyage—the percentage of the carry.) Meanwhile, the captain would negotiate a percentage of the whole investment—say, 2 percent—to cover the cost of buying food and supplies for the crew. This "two and twenty" structure would eventually be copied and pasted for investing in startups.

Investors tried many other business models, but "two and twenty" would carry the day. Over time, the venture capital industry developed the now-canonical rule for management fees, and the term "carry" is still widely used. But today it's being used to chase unicorns rather than whales.

UNTAPPED COMPANIES: BIG FUNDS LEAVE BIG GAPS

"Two and twenty" is hardly the only thing wrong with the venture capital process, but it's one example of a structural problem that makes all our other problems more difficult to solve. In the introduction we spoke about the Procrustean bed—the danger of forcing a square peg into a round hole even if we scrape off the edges in the process. Venture capital has been stuck in the Procrustean bed of "two and twenty" since its early days, and the scraps of mangled edges are starting to pile up high on the floor.

But the process that worked so well for the titans of the whaling industry is causing us to miss out on companies today. A 2014 *Harvard Business Review* article, "Venture Capitalists Get Paid Well to Lose Money," illustrates how the "two and twenty," one-size-fits-all model can result in misaligned incentives and a blind spot for innovation.[16]

To start, fund managers always make 2 percent fees on their "assets under management"—regardless of the fund size. If the fund is large, managers make good money regardless of whether the companies succeed (the median partner's salary at the average venture capital firm in the United States is $750,000).[17] So managers have an incentive to build as large a fund as possible, and that's where the problem starts: if you've got a $1 billion fund, you need to decide how to spend large amounts of money very quickly.

According to a 2013 World Economic Forum report, it takes the same amount of time to conduct "due diligence"—deep research investigating investment quality—on a $10 million investment as it does on a $100 million investment. So large investors will almost always go for the larger deal—or the one that fits patterns that are easier to understand.[18]

The two-and-twenty structure encourages investors to raise as large a fund as possible, meaning they are more likely to overlook ideas that seem "too small." Let's get back to Jerry Nemorin. When he was originally raising money for LendStreet, he noticed that very few venture capitalists understood the problem of private debt refinancing. "In the Valley," he said, "people are looking to solve their own problems, looking for things to build for the top 10 or 1 percent." When you've got major incentives to raise a large fund and a serious time pressure to deploy capital, you likely won't take the time to learn about debt refinancing. This oversight is unintentional, but it means that ideas outside the mainstream struggle to raise money.

INUNDATED BY IDEAS, WE LACK THE TOOLS TO EVALUATE THE BEST

The problem with innovation does not come from a lack of ideas. I've probably seen, in my career, over five thousand examples of "Famous Startup X for Industry Y"—think "Uber for tennis coaches" or "Kickstarter for nonprofits." If you've ever played the game Mad Libs, you can generate a hundred ideas in an hour.

Most venture capital firms I know hear about a thousand new ideas a year. According to a recent Harvard Business School study, the average firm spends a total of three minutes and forty-four seconds evaluating each pitch deck. Out of those thousand ideas, a firm will invest in a dozen at most.[19]

Humans are genetically predisposed, when we're facing information overload, to save time by making rules. This has been in our DNA from the beginning: animals with big teeth are bad; water is good. Gerd Gigerenzer, of the Max Planck Institute in Berlin, calls decision-making rules "fast and frugal" heuristics: we can't possibly analyze all the information in front of us, so we develop shortcuts.[20]

But these shortcuts exclude most of our best ideas. Why does almost 80 percent of startup investment go to just three US states? Because that's where the money lives. Only four of the top twenty-five most active venture capital firms in the country were head-quartered outside New York City, Boston, and San Francisco.[21] Why does the majority of startup investment go to founders who are white, male, and from connected networks? Because that's who investors know from their networks and their personal lives. We all have biases that affect our decision-making, but as psychologist Khatera Sahibzada puts it, "Because of the pressure and uncertainties investors face in making decisions, any bias factor can be amplified and become detrimental."[22]

We're much more likely to see millions go to a company that delivers food faster to yuppies in urban areas than one that helps struggling rural families simply put food on the table. Because venture funds are under extreme pressure to deliver quick profits to investors, they prioritize short-term value capture over long-term value creation.

We'll talk more about the people and places we're missing in chapter 3, but first let's take a final look at what makes it so difficult to innovate the process around how we innovate.

IS BIGGER ALWAYS BETTER?

Diane Mulcahy of the Ewing Marion Kauffman Foundation analyzed thousands of venture capital funds and their perfor-mance and found one surprising result: over time, smaller funds significantly outperform larger funds. In the banking and asset management industry, people often think that bigger is better, but in the venture capital process, that isn't necessarily true.[23]

We may have set ourselves up for failure. Venture capital partners have an economic interest in raising massive funds. But the size of the fund is often negatively correlated with the returns that it provides to investors. This isn't because the partners aren't smart or well intentioned. It's because partners have lots of money to deploy quickly. And entrepreneurs who aren't in the system may die on the vine.

Not all venture capitalists think that bigger is better. Many venture capital funds have built the right fund, for the right size, to solve the right problem, rather than raise as much money as possible. Fred Wilson, founder of Union Square Ventures, is one of the most successful and thoughtful venture capitalists in the industry. He's invested in Tumblr, Lending Club, Foursquare, and a dozen other companies whose services you may have used. Wilson has kept the size of each subsequent fund at about $150 million, which is small for a venture capital fund. In a blog post after the closing of his last fund, Wilson wrote, "The goal of VC fund economics is to incent the partners to focus on carry and not on current cash compensation. . . . [The system] can break down as the dollars under management get larger and larger and the management fees turn into huge numbers. We have purposely kept USV small to avoid that. And I think that has been a good decision for us." Union Square Ventures could have $2 billion under management, based on their performance, but has decided to stay small in order to innovate.[24]

Venture capitalists Brad Feld and David Cohen cofounded a group called Techstars that provides small funding to batches of companies through a program known as an accelerator. Techstars now provides funding in the $100,000 range to groups of companies in Boulder, Austin, and New York, and has recently arranged partnerships with Ford in Detroit and with Target in Minneapolis.

Like Union Square Ventures, Techstars could raise a $2 billion global fund but has decided to invest in new ideas through a hyper-local model.

Globally, investors Dave McClure and Christine Tsai founded a group called 500 Startups in the Bay Area, which has launched $10 to $20 million micro-funds around the world (as 500 Luchadores in Latin America, 500 Kulfi in India, 500 TukTuks in Thailand, and so on). Instead of setting up a Mexico City, Bangalore, or Bangkok office, McClure and Tsai recruit local fund managers, seed their work with a small base investment, and rely on those fund managers to invest in the ideas they can see on the ground.

Thinking with intellectual curiosity and self-awareness about *how* we invest is critical, because the way we structure our investments shapes *who* and *where* we invest. And as we'll see in the next chapter, if we don't build systems that are accessible to the best ideas, we'll miss most of them.

CHAPTER 3

People and Place:
It's Who You Know

*(Or When It's Easier to Raise $800 Million with a
Fake Product Than $100,000 with a Real One)*

You miss 100 percent of the shots you don't take.
    —Wayne Gretzky

The best luck always happens to people who don't need it.
    —Robert Penn Warren, *All the King's Men*

Elizabeth Holmes was born in Washington, DC, to a family that moved in powerful circles, as her father was a high-ranking government official. As a nineteen-year-old undergrad at Stanford University, she created a wearable patch that could adjust the dosage of drugs delivered to a patient. She then turned the patch into a full blood test that promised to do something revolutionary: extract blood with a single pinprick.

Elizabeth sometimes dressed in a black turtleneck, like Apple founder Steve Jobs. She started her company, Theranos, in a strip mall near Stanford's campus, blocks from where Facebook and Google started, and began attending conferences to talk about her blood test invention. Partly through these conferences and partly through her school and family connections, she was quickly able to get the backing of dozens of prominent people—not only in venture capital but in academia and politics as well. She filled her investor base and advisory board with VIPs like former secretaries of state Henry Kissinger and George Shultz, current and former secretaries of defense James Mattis and William Perry, and billionaires like Secretary of Education Betsy DeVos and Oracle founder Larry Ellison. Within a few years, Theranos was valued at nearly $10 billion.[25]

It would seem that by the standards of venture capital, Theranos was a smashing success: Holmes raised $800 million and was, on paper, one of the youngest self-made billionaires in the world. There was only one problem: Theranos's product didn't work. The blood test results were never scientifically validated, and in 2016, the Centers for Medicaid and Medicare Services revoked the company's operating certificate and banned the founders from scientific labs for two years, causing Theranos to lose nearly 100 percent of its value.[26]

Let's compare Theranos's story with that of another company, founded around the same time. This one was founded by an Asian immigrant, opened its doors in rural Kentucky, and aimed to make money by harvesting fish.

Lula Luu was born in South Vietnam to parents who fought alongside US troops in the Vietnam War. After the war, Lula's father disappeared and her mother smuggled her children onto a container ship bound for America and they settled in Oak Ridge, Tennessee.

Lula's mother worked multiple minimum-wage jobs, and Lula grew up in the care of the women in the community. She earned a scholarship to the University of Kentucky, where she earned her PhD in nutrition. In her dissertation field work, she studied a problem she understood plagued both Vietnam and rural Appalachia: diabetes.

After graduate school, Lula moved to Louisiana to study how extreme poverty contributed to diabetes, while her partner, John, studied the mental health of the rural population. They spent years interviewing fishermen and shrimpers in the Gulf of Mexico, and one outlier kept catching their attention: Asian carp. In the Mississippi River watershed, Asian carp is an invasive species, native to Asia, and is considered one of the region's biggest environmental threats. It's also plentiful. Lula and John saw a business opportunity. They bought carp from underemployed fishermen and hired people in halfway houses, ex-cons returning from prison, and women who had suffered domestic abuse to process the fish and sell them.

They started to make a profit and soon moved the business to cleaner waters in Paducah, Kentucky. They now run a company called Fin Gourmet, which follows the same business model: fishermen catch carp, employees in rural Kentucky make a living wage processing the fish, and Fin Gourmet sells it to mainstream markets. In 2015, they grossed $1.5 million and are growing impressively.

Village Capital invested $50,000 in Fin Gourmet, but despite impressive revenue growth, they have struggled to get more resources. A representative from the US Department of Commerce promised Lula and John money if they presented an "ironclad business plan," but didn't respond to Fin Gourmet's follow-up calls. Another international fish sourcing company committed over $2 million in investment and showed up for a Fin Gourmet ribbon cutting with Kentucky's lieutenant governor. But when it came time to wire the money, the company went radio silent.

Why does Fin Gourmet struggle to raise money while Theranos succeeded?

In the last chapter, we talked about how the people who are investing in innovation have incentives to see what we call "hockey stick" growth—very quick, up-and-to-the-right returns. To play it safe, they rely on the types of patterns that make Elizabeth

Holmes's biomedical company in Silicon Valley a lot more compelling to most investors than Lula Luu's fish company in Paducah, Kentucky—or, for that matter, Jerry Nemorin's consumer credit company in Charlottesville, Virginia.

Elizabeth Holmes in many ways seemed to be breaking the mold—a young, female entrepreneur in the male-dominated field of science raising gobs of cash. But even when we think we're looking past blind spots, we can be blinded in other ways. You might say that Theranos raised more money because, at the end of the day, it was a bigger market opportunity. But remember: Theranos was raising money on evidence that the Department of Health and Human Services said wasn't real! Other "unicorns," such as HR benefits firm Zenefits and Just Mayo manufacturer Hampton Creek, came under similar scrutiny for representing product traction based on statistics that were at best ill-informed and at worst fabricated. Theranos's fundamentals weren't scrutinized simply because of the patterns the company fit. Silicon Valley lore is filled with stories of entrepreneurs playing fast and loose with reality—but the money keeps coming.

IT'S TOUGH TO BOOTSTRAP IF YOU DON'T HAVE BOOTS

If you're unable to raise the money you need, investors often say you should "bootstrap"—self-fund your company. After all, Wilbur and Orville Wright bootstrapped their "flying machine" through profits from a bicycle repair shop. Steve Jobs and Steve Wozniak created the first personal computer with their parents' savings. Indeed, the majority of founders don't raise money for their ideas; they begin with personal savings. But most founders don't have enough cash on hand to start their dream company—particularly since the Great Recession of 2008. Nor do founders necessarily have wealth in the form of home equity: the US home ownership rate in 2016 fell to its lowest since 1967.[27]

To add to the problem, student debt has grown over 100 percent in the last twenty years, particularly among graduates from for-profit and two-year colleges, which low-income people disproportionately attend.[28] And founders who are in debt are less likely to start their own business after graduation.[29]

The Kauffman Foundation estimates that the average cost of starting a business is $30,000. Most entrepreneurs in most places—men and women, urban and rural, all races and classes—can't afford that. The median level of wealth holdings for African-Americans and Latinos is under $9,000 (compared to over $110,000 for white families—more than ten times as high!). Rural families and veterans also can't afford the basic table stakes—indeed, most Americans aren't even in the conversation to begin with.[30]

Other traditional sources of capital are drying up as well. According to the Federal Reserve Bank of Kansas City, community banks are most likely to lend to small businesses.[31] Yet the number of community banks has declined 41 percent since the financial crisis.[32] It turns out that bootstrapping is tougher than it sounds.

THE MYTH OF MERITOCRACY

In this chapter we'll take a closer look at the blind spots that cause investors to miss out on places, people, and types of companies that simply don't fit the prevailing patterns. The best investors are quite aware of these blind spots. Paul Graham, the founder of YCombinator, arguably one of the most influential early-stage investors in Silicon Valley, once joked, "I can be tricked by anyone who looks like Mark Zuckerberg." But as Graham reflected, he asked, "Could anyone be so naive as to think that resembling Zuck would be enough to make a founder succeed?"

But it happens, again and again. I regularly hear venture capitalists say, "He's a great guy" as a shorthand way to convey "He's part of a tribe I understand." And on the flip side, I hear about investors meeting with an unfamiliar entrepreneur and saying, "That was a very *interesting* meeting," which is often code for "I don't understand what you are trying to do, and I'm not going to try."

Let's start by looking at place, because I also hear about investors who won't even look at a company that would require them to take a connecting flight. Indeed, the average distance between a VC firm and the companies it invests in is eighty miles. So what about people living anywhere else, people with big ideas?

Where you are

Peter Thiel is a Silicon Valley venture capitalist, cofounder of PayPal, board member of Facebook, and author of *Zero to One*, a popular book about startups. Thiel tends to think in absolutes, as in this piece of advice he once offered to entrepreneurs: "Competition is for losers. Build a monopoly." In Thiel's world, even cities are winner-take-all. He once said, "If you are a very talented person, you have a choice: You either go to New York or you go to Silicon Valley."[33]

This type of thinking is precisely why investors pool their resources in companies like Theranos, Zenefits, and Hampton Creek without looking at the fundamentals—and why companies like LendStreet and Fin Gourmet are often overlooked.

Thiel is not alone in this winner-take-all perspective. Sam Altman, the president of YCombinator, is a good example of how most venture capitalists look at geography. He believes that moving to San Francisco "increases the value of a startup at least ten times"—in fact, his firm won't invest in startups that don't move to San Francisco, saying, "We would not be doing them a favor by not making them move."[34] If you're a founder, you might want to pay attention. Jerry Nemorin did: he had to move to Cupertino to raise money.

For entrepreneurs living in Silicon Valley, Brooklyn, or Boston's Seaport District, it's relatively easy to raise money. Since the mid-'90s, funding for startups has increased by 300 percent in California, New York, and Massachusetts.[35] Year after year, more than three-quarters of startup investment from the private sector goes to those three states. And, as of the beginning of 2017, some 41 percent of unicorns continue to be based in—you've probably already guessed where.[36]

An economist might say, "Capital flows to its most productive uses—I'm not surprised that capital flows to the most thriving cities." But the data wouldn't back up this counterargument: despite the disparity in capital, there is no statistically significant difference in financial performance across states.[37]

This idea hurts capital-starved areas: entrepreneurs spend far more time fundraising than building their business. I once spoke with a Silicon Valley investor about why a company in the Midwest was having such a tough time raising money. I told him that the average investor in the Midwest, in my experience, took about six months to make a decision. "I would be shot if I took that long," said my friend, "and I'd never get in a good deal again." If an investor in Silicon Valley mistreats a founder, it hurts their reputation: there is more money than investment opportunities in Silicon Valley, and other talented founders won't want to work with that investor. But in cash-starved areas, whether it's Minneapolis or Nairobi, investors can take advantage of founders and not face any consequences. Future investment opportunities will still come their way.

This blind spot leads us to miss out on great ideas and untapped markets. Just as in real estate, a market frenzy over a specific location can cause prices to rise dramatically—and open up opportunities where no one else is looking. For instance, in recent years, if you invested in a company outside New York, Boston, or San Francisco at similar stages, the value—what you paid for your shares in the company—would have been at a 35 percent discount compared to peer companies in the "Big Three."

When measuring eighteen thousand investments over the last twenty years, economist Pat Scruggs noted that the average venture capital investment in the three VC-heavy states was $12 million, and the average investment in the other states was $6 million. In 2013, ExactTarget, a digital marketing company in Indianapolis, was acquired by Salesforce for over $2 billion—the same price a company would pay for a Silicon Valley startup—even though it cost a fraction of that amount to build. And when companies such as Under Armour issue stock in the public markets, investors don't pay less because the company is in Baltimore.[38]

If you invest outside the hotbeds where everyone else is, and the company succeeds, on average you'll pay 35 percent less to get the same end financial result.[39]

Who you know

Place is just one example of the many shortcuts that venture capitalists take to vet companies. "He's a great guy" is another one. In the venture capital process, who you know often matters more than how good your idea is. In order to manage the constant stream of startups coming their way, investors often rely on "warm introductions" from friends and colleagues. For instance, angel investor Chris Sacca decided that his firm, Lowercase Capital, was going to "focus exclusively on deals that come to us through our trusted network of friends and colleagues whom we admire."[40] Sacca, by all accounts, seems like a thoughtful, kind, and inquisitive guy, but most people don't know someone who knows Chris

Sacca and can tell him what a "great guy" they are. But Chris Sacca has perhaps found the most value in his investments from more unusual places. In the spring of 2017, he announced his retirement from day-to-day investing, but talked passionately about the kinds of things he was going to continue to be involved in. For example, he's proudly backed Tala, led by Shivani Siroya, a leader in mobile banking in Africa. He's also backed Backstage Capital, a fund led by an African American woman, Arlan Hamilton, who touts as a metric of success the number of founders that the fund learns about via cold e-mail.

What you look like

Let's say you do get an introduction to someone with money. How likely are you to succeed? It often depends on what you look like.

To start, an investor is more likely to put money into a company run by someone who looks like they do. According to a 2014 study by Babson College, venture capital firms with female partners are three times as likely to invest in companies with female CEOs, though at the time, only 6 percent of partners at venture firms were women.[41]

A 2014 Harvard Business School study found that male entrepreneurs were 60 percent more likely to receive a funding prize than female entrepreneurs—even when both male and female promoters pitched the same ideas. The male entrepreneurs whom investors deemed physically attractive were 36 percent more likely to be successful; for women, their looks had no effect on the success of their pitches.[42] Wharton's Laura Huang drew similar conclusions in her article "Who's the Most Attractive Investment Opportunity of All? Good-Looking Men."[43] She found that among businesses with similar fundamentals and markets, attractive people got funded more than unattractive people, and men were funded more than women. Moreover, the same idea pitched with a man's voice got considerably more interest than when it was pitched with a woman's voice.

Not surprisingly, racial biases play a factor, too. In a study by economists Marianne Bertrand and Sendhil Mullainathan, identical resumes with the names "Greg" and "Emily" were sent to employers alongside resumes with the names "Jamal" and "Lakisha." Despite identical resumes, Greg and Emily received 50 percent more callbacks than Jamal and Lakisha.[44]

What you're building

Many times, investors don't understand the problems entrepreneurs are solving, because they don't have the same experiences.

Sara Blakely is the founder of Spanx, an undergarment company for women. She often talks about her first attempts to sell to a major department store, where the buyers simply didn't understand the product. She finally decided, midway through her sales pitch, to change into her product to give buyers a "before and after" view, looking more attractive when wearing her product. Only then did the buyers—mostly male—understand what Spanx was and why it would be important.[45] So many women found the product important and valuable that Sara Blakely is now the youngest self-made billionaire in the United States.

UNTAPPED MARKETS: THE POWER OF LIVED EXPERIENCE

Blind spots cause investors to miss not only companies but also entire markets of people. Too many investors stick to a narrow range of ideas shaped by their own echo chamber—rather than a real understanding of customer needs.

Jerry Nemorin developed a powerful idea because he knew what it was like to live without credit, and he is gaining traction with a market of people struggling with the same problem. Sara Blakely created an idea that women found valuable (to the tune of billions of dollars), but (mostly) male venture capitalists and buyers didn't understand.

Instead of focusing primarily on pedigree, investors should actively search for entrepreneurs who are solving real-world problems that they are intimately familiar with. Village Capital invested in a company called Student Loan Genius, started by Tony Aguilar, an immigrant's kid from Pecos, Texas. Student Loan Genius, a 401(k) for student loans, helps employers match their employees' loan repayment as a workforce benefit. When Tony started fundraising for his company, investors asked, "What's the catch? Why hasn't anyone started this company before?" Tony reminded them that most startup founders don't have huge amounts of personal debt, so it was not an issue they were aware of and looking to solve.

If we look for innovators who have experience with important problems, we get better solutions. This not only results in more impactful investments, it also offers a competitive advantage to forward-thinking investors. After all, from a customer's perspective, it doesn't matter what a company's founder looks like or where they went to school, only whether they make a great product.

When we get different founders in the conversation, we see a new pattern: instead of what Jerry Nemorin calls "my-world problems," these companies are also solving "real-world problems." This is not a coincidence, as we'll see in the next chapter.

CHAPTER 4

THE TWO-POCKET MENTALITY

How Short-Term Thinking Sets Us Up for Long-Term Failure

Today's culture of quarterly earnings hysteria is totally contrary to the long-term approach we need.
—Larry Fink, CEO, BlackRock (excerpt from annual letter to shareholders, February 2016)

Real generosity to the future lies in giving all to the present.
—Albert Camus

Jim Sorenson was in trouble. In the late 1990s, his company had developed video conferencing solutions (essentially an early version of Skype or FaceTime) that were able to transmit video from point to point over the Internet bandwidth limitations at that time. Sorenson Communications, located in Salt Lake City, attracted substantial interest in the dot-com boom of the late 1990s. But in 2002, the day after Jim Sorenson received his commitment for venture capital funding, the dot-com bubble burst. The funding Jim needed evaporated, and he faced a difficult decision. At a time when the company was losing a million dollars a month, should he close the company, laying off thousands of people, or find another way forward?

Jim's brother-in-law, who is deaf, approached Jim with an idea: a new technology called video relay service (VRS) that could help the deaf. Until this time, the deaf population in the United States could communicate long-distance only by using a relatively archaic system that wasn't much more efficient than the telegraph. VRS made it possible for the deaf to communicate in their own language, American Sign Language (ASL), through a remote ASL interpreter over the Internet in real time. This allowed deaf people to set up doctor's appointments, order a pizza, or call a hearing client just as hearing people do in everyday life. The only problem: the video technology required so much bandwidth at the time that most could not use it.

Jim's brother-in-law wondered whether Sorenson Communications' technology could be put to use in enabling a better solution for VRS. After some research, Jim realized that the answer was yes—and that this opportunity could save the company. Having spent almost a decade developing a high-quality, reliable, low-cost Internet video conferencing solution, Sorenson Communications was well positioned to offer a much better service than even established telecommunications competitors like AT&T and Sprint. Moreover, to incentivize private-sector service providers, the FCC was reimbursing the providers for VRS usage at a rate of over $17 per connected minute.

Jim seized the opportunity. Sorenson Communications installed a small video conferencing unit in the homes of deaf people across the country, free of charge. With the push of a button, the VP-100 would connect deaf individuals across the country to ASL interpreters, who would then relay deaf-to-hearing conversations seamlessly and reliably in real time. The deaf community called Sorenson Communications "the Alexander Graham Bell for the deaf."

Sorenson Communications' business grew like crazy, achieving 70 percent market share within a year. The company now employs nearly ten thousand people, providing millions of deaf people with access to communication. And with communication comes opportunity: deaf people who use VRS are four times more likely to be employed than those who do not.

HOW ONE-POCKET COMPANIES OUTPERFORM TWO-POCKET ONES

Most companies, when they talk about their "contribution to society," mention their philanthropic work or their "corporate social responsibility" budget. Like Jane in the introduction, they have two separate pockets, one for business, and one for philanthropy. The problem with this model: the "philanthropy pocket" represents only a tiny fraction of the company's resources.

In the mid-2000s, Jim sold Sorenson Communications for hundreds of millions of dollars. Having built a company with massive social impact and attractive financial returns, he became one of the world's most prominent one-pocket thinkers. He endowed the Sorenson Impact Center at the University of Utah to give students experience understanding how to invest in and build businesses that are generating both profit and impact, and he has worked closely with dozens of entrepreneurs around the world (including chairing the board at Village Capital).

Jim's success with Sorenson Communications saved and created thousands of jobs, helped millions of deaf and hard of hearing people, and led to millions of dollars invested in new startups. And the idea that saved the company didn't come from consultants or the leadership team—it came from a team member from a disadvantaged population who saw potential in a completely transformative application of the company's product.

Many people describe their personal philanthropy as "giving back." But as eBay founder Pierre Omidyar once said, "Giving back implies, at one point, that you were taking. We're dissociating what we do from what we value, and it's becoming very difficult to improve the world as a result."[46]

WHY DO WE DISSOCIATE *WHAT* WE DO FROM *WHY* WE DO IT?

Two-pocket thinking is a blind spot that limits our ability to have a successful society. Most two-pocket thinkers believe that their two pockets balance each other—that if they spend their whole life making money in the "business pocket," but at the end of their life give it all to charity, at some point it will all even out. But the numbers don't back up that idea.

You likely know the world's biggest foundations: Gates, Rockefeller, Ford. Here's what most people don't know: incredibly, foundations are only required to give 5 percent of their assets to charitable causes each year.

If I become wealthy and create a million-dollar foundation, I'm eligible for a million-dollar tax break—but I'm only required to grant $50,000 dollars every twelve months.

What happens to the other 95 percent? Most of the time, foundations will hire an asset manager or big investment bank to invest it in the capital markets—just like if they had never started the foundation in the first place. Sometimes these investments can even run counter to the foundation's mission: if, for example, you are a foundation that supports economic opportunity in distressed areas, you might be surprised to find out that your endowment is invested in a public company that is automating, offshoring, or otherwise eliminating jobs while paying its management incredible sums of money. Harvard has a $35 billion endowment and is only required to spend $1.75 billion of that a year on education of students, faculty research, and more (at a school where tuition, room, and board is $63,000 a year). If you give $1 million to Harvard, only $50,000 a year is required to go toward the school's charitable purpose; the remainder is invested in the capital markets.

If we live in a two-pocket world, where business has no responsibility for what happens in society, we're fighting a losing battle.

Public companies that trade in the global capital markets hold $200 trillion in wealth; trillions more are likely privately held. In the philanthropy world, the value of all of the charitable foundations in the world combined add up to less than $1 trillion—and as we just saw, only 5 percent of the capital is being spent each year; the other 95 percent is invested in the capital markets! If the "what's good for business" pocket were the size of the Statue of Liberty, the "what's good for society" pocket would be the size of a grasshopper.

Most people today subscribe to two-pocket thinking. Investors, CEOs, and board members of the *Fortune* 500 would say that the goal of this $200 trillion is to maximize shareholder value. Indeed, Nobel Prize–winning economist Milton Friedman's theory of shareholder value says, "The social responsibility of business is to increase profits."[47]

But before Milton Friedman, conventional economic wisdom was more one-pocket. Adam Smith's pioneering theory of economics, *The Wealth of Nations,* talks about supply, demand, and the "invisible hand" of the market—but these days, we'd do better to look more closely at his lesser-known companion text, *The Theory of Moral Sentiments.* Whereas *The Wealth of Nations* talks about information, or how economics works, *The Theory of Moral Sentiments* talks about the values behind decisions, or why economics should work in the first place. This quotation from the latter volume sums it up: "How selfish soever man may be supposed, there are evidently some principles in his nature, which interest him in the fortune of others, and render their happiness necessary to him."[48]

I had an economics professor at the University of Virginia who said, "Decisions are a combination of information and values. This class teaches you the information. You have to develop your own code of values." One-pocket thinking combines the two in a single effort; two-pocket thinking decouples them. Entrepreneurs are required, in a two-pocket world, to maximize profits—and then can take care of society with what's left over. This division becomes a battle, and society loses. And in the longer run, investors lose, too.

MORAL LICENSING

In 2013, YCombinator announced that it would begin funding nonprofits with its support of Watsi, an online platform that lets anyone make a contribution to help people worldwide pay for healthcare costs. YCombinator founder Paul Graham said, "I've never been so excited about anything we've funded."[49] Yet as of 2017, nonprofits represent less than 1 percent of what YCombinator has funded.

The psychological blind spot known as "moral licensing" may play a role here. This subconscious phenomenon allows us to give ourselves disproportionate credit for doing one good thing while ignoring other consequences of our behavior. In a 2010 description of the phenomenon, *Washington Post* writer Michael Rosenwald describes a series of examples: "We go to the gym—and take the elevator to the second floor. . . . We drive SUVs to see Al Gore's speeches on global warming."[50] In the same way, perhaps funding Watsi and just a few other nonprofits gives YCombinator moral license to ignore the impacts, good or bad, of all the other companies it funds.

Moreover, by funding a few nonprofits, YCombinator and others perpetuate two-pocket thinking. If, for example, YCombinator announced that they were going to fund only businesses that address problems important to society, I hypothesize that you'd see a lot more Harvard MBAs and Stanford computer scientists become one-pocket thinkers. I also think you'd see a more level playing field for people who come from different experiences— entrepreneurs in the middle of the country who better understand energy and agriculture, perhaps, or people who grew up in communities with struggling public education systems.

Moral licensing and the universal basic income: is this the future we want?

Moral licensing may also be to blame for building an innovation economy that kills more solutions than it promotes. In 2016, YCombinator announced an experiment in universal basic income, an idea that has gained substantial traction among Silicon Valley thinkers in the last five years. The core idea is that every citizen would get a minimum paycheck—say, $15,000 per year.

In the future, YCombinator's Sam Altman says, we will have "smaller and smaller numbers of people creating more and more of the wealth. And we need a new solution for the people not creating most of the wealth—many of the minimum-wage jobs are going to get innovated away anyway." The people without jobs will be an "idle class"—and the obvious conclusion, to Altman, "is that the government will just have to give *these people* money." (Emphasis mine.) And you wonder why political candidates on both sides are tapping into anti-elitist anger with great success.

In the universal basic income proposal, the YCombinator team posits that Silicon Valley's wonderful creations will create an incredible amount of wealth even while these companies will put a lot of people out of work.

Paul Graham, Sam Altman, and others are right that the loss of jobs due to automation is a serious problem that we need to solve as a society. For example, if self-driving cars are commercialized in the United States, truck and taxi drivers will be out of work. In twenty-nine states in 2015, "truck driver" was the most common job, and it is one of the few solid middle-class jobs that one can have and maintain without a college degree.[51] With three million truck drivers, this is not an insignificant part of the US workforce.

You could take this to its logical (and cynical) conclusion and say that the rest of the world will eventually be out of work and become a burden on the enlightened few. They'll storm the gates of Silicon Valley's kingdom, and the resulting social unrest will be an unfortunate distraction to the wonders of artificial intelligence, research into extending life past the age of 120, and other great wonders of modern technology. The universal basic income will keep "these people" at bay, serving as a consolation prize for the people who don't win.

It's not necessarily a bad thing to explore the feasibility of universal basic income. But I see the focus on this one idea as the "obvious conclusion" providing us moral license to ignore other ideas.[52] When we hyper-focus on one too-simple idea like universal basic income, we ignore that everything we do has repercussions—for good or for ill.

BUILDING COMPANIES TO FLIP, NOT TO LAST

Moral licensing aside, two-pocket thinking has contributed to an unfortunate trend that makes startup investing look more like real estate investing: building companies to flip them as fast as possible.

The financialization of the economy means that what we invest in is no longer entrepreneurs making goods and producing services, but the creation and leverage of intermediaries who extract tolls, rent, and capital gains. The most valuable companies in the world, from Amazon to Walmart to Facebook to Google, do not produce goods or services but instead are trading companies who mediate financial transactions between producers and consumers.

The way that many people practice the venture capital process gives investors incentive to extract value from payments and capital gains rather than create a truly breakthrough innovation. Today, when venture capitalists invest in a company, one of the first questions they ask is "What's your exit strategy?" That's because the way they most commonly make money is through an "exit"—typically, when a larger firm acquires the startup. Case in point: The handful of investors in Instagram did quite well when Facebook bought the company thirteen months after its initial public offering (IPO) for $1 billion.

Yet to build a truly transformative company, you need much longer than that to succeed. In 1991, only 3 percent of Americans had ever been online; by the year 2000, nearly 27 million Americans subscribed to America Online's service alone. AOL founder Steve Case often calls the company "an overnight success that took ten years." Microsoft likewise took ten years to reach its IPO. Hewlett-Packard, Silicon Valley's original innovator, took nearly twenty years. Nike took twenty-five.

The simple fact is that selling YouTube to Google or Instagram to Facebook realizes success more quickly than investing in a clean energy company that will require years of research and development, or a healthcare company that needs to wait for FDA approval. "Investment" for the short term is capturing value quickly. "Investment" for the long term is creating value that lasts. Though, as I'll argue in later chapters, it is possible to achieve both.

ONE-POCKET THINKING AS AN UNTAPPED INVESTMENT STRATEGY

Two-pocket thinking is seductive, but wrong. Just like corporate CEOs who argue that one-pocket thinking would break their fiduciary duty to shareholders, or foundations that argue they cannot risk their endowment, venture capitalists often argue that investing with purpose goes against their basic job.

This argument contains a faulty assumption: that if I integrate "what's good for society" into my business decisions, I'll lose money. The evidence doesn't support this. In a 2014 study,

Cambridge Associates illustrated how funds that intentionally integrated social impact and financial returns performed similarly in developed markets and outperformed in emerging markets. And a 2015 Wharton study showed that smaller funds that integrated purpose likewise outperformed those that didn't.

Why are we settling for just short-term gains? Especially when it's quite possibly bad for financial returns in the long run.

THE ILLUMINATORS

In the first part of this book, I've tried to diagnose the blind spots that society creates. We're not always directing time, attention, and resources to the people, places, and problems that might truly improve society—and make solid returns in the process.

In the next section, I'll introduce you to what I call the Illuminators, an emerging group of people and firms that are trying to shine a light on these blind spots. I'll also tell the story of Village Capital, and how I joined this conversation.

A note: You may notice in the coming chapters that a lot of the people I highlight in the coming chapters have names like Bob, Dan, and Steve. And they're all white guys. Power dynamics are real in the innovation economy. The people who are in a position to change the system are often those who are already running things—and in the case of venture capital and business, that's still mostly white men. Most of the largest investors in this book, and in society, are white guys in American cities—because most of the people who have access to resources, myself included, are white guys living in American cities.

As you think about these Illuminators, keep in mind that changing who gets access to capital will change the conversation intergenerationally. I always appreciate the thoughts of Freada Kapor Klein, of Kapor Capital, on this topic. Freada points out that in the short term, we need to be more inclusive about who we hire and who we invest in, because, as we'll see in later chapters, evidence abounds that diverse teams perform better and can help us get past blind spots. If Ex-Big Successful Company Employee (She's ex-Google! He's ex-Facebook!) has a competitive advantage in the hiring process, Freada often says, and the successful companies aren't diverse companies, we're not creating opportunities for people who aren't already in the system. If we have more startup founders from nontraditional backgrounds today, we'll have more diverse decision-makers in the next generation.

PART II

THE EMERGING
MOVEMENT

Illuminating the Blind Spots

When I woke up just after dawn on September 28, 1928,
I certainly didn't plan to revolutionise all medicine by
discovering the world's first antibiotic, or bacteria killer. But
I suppose that was exactly what I did.
    —Sir Alexander Fleming, who accidentally discovered
        penicillin when he forgot to clean up his laboratory

It's not who you know, it's who you get to know.
    —Chris Matthews, *Hardball*

I f an entrepreneur is building a company that has an intentional
positive impact on society, odds are good there's a line back to
Bob Pattillo in there somewhere. Bob is a sandy-haired, bearded
entrepreneur who is usually wearing bright-orange Crocs. He
carries a notebook around that he calls his "inkling pipeline"—
different ideas or inklings that could become companies one day.
His title in his company's directory is "Inkler." Bob has a knack for
overcoming blind spots in order to see ideas that no one else has.
I'm using his story to start this section because Bob's success is a
result of him overcoming these blind spots—and he's had a few
big wins that provide lessons for all of us.

Bob's first big win came from investing in unexpected parts
of the country. A seventh-generation Georgian, Bob started his
career working in his family's construction business, selling warehouses to large companies such as Target. When the real estate
market crashed at the end of the 1980s, the family company's
profits were tanking, and the future of industrial real estate looked
bleak. Experts blamed economic cycles and cautioned the industry to "wait and see," but Bob hit the road and started talking to
his customers. He noticed a trend: customers were still spending money, but instead of buying buildings, they were using new
supply-chain technology to build their own.

Bob decided to take a massive risk and build new sites "on spec"—that is, without a purchaser signed. To make the risk affordable, he started buying real estate not in New York or Los Angeles but near undervalued transportation hubs such as Louisville, Kentucky, the seventh busiest airport in the world. Bob's competitors kept investing in big properties in big cities, and they kept losing. From 1986 to 1992, the value of the commercial real estate market dropped 43 percent, a larger decline than the industry would experience during the Great Recession. But Bob was investing in different places from his competitors, and his Pattillo Properties spec warehouses took off. A small local business became the eighth largest real estate developer in the country. Bob understood that when you're investing where no one else is, you can outperform those who are following the same patterns.

Bob's second big win came as a result of becoming one of the world's first "one-pocket thinkers." At age thirty-eight, Bob was one of the most successful young CEOs in America, but he felt that something was missing in his life. One day, while playing pool with Steven Rockefeller, he learned about a Bangladeshi professor named Muhammad Yunus. In the 1970s Dr. Yunus had started giving small loans to entrepreneurs whom banks would never lend to—craftspeople, farmers, mostly women. He went on to win the Nobel Peace Prize for this concept of "microfinance," and through his Grameen Bank popularized the idea of the "village bank." Around the world, peer groups of entrepreneurs would meet regularly, share their business plans, and then decide among themselves who would get a loan. Bob Pattillo learned that these loans were repaying at over a 99 percent rate.

Bob had already started a charitable foundation, and he began making grants to nonprofit microfinance banks. But an unusual conversation on one trip to Bangladesh opened his eyes to the potential for something more lasting. As a philanthropist, Bob had almost never had a conversation with a grantee that felt as if they were on equal footing. Bob would give a grant to a school or a nonprofit, and when it came time to visit, it felt like "show and tell": people would just tell him how great it was. When he visited his first village bank, though, the power dynamic was different. He asked one of the female entrepreneurs what her dreams were. She started talking about what she wanted for her family, her business, and her country. Then she turned to Bob and, with steely confidence, said, "What about you? What are your dreams?" Bob was floored. He saw himself as a partner, not a benefactor. "If our bank stopped making loans today, this woman would still be confident and successful. I saw a world of respect and trust."

It occurred to Bob that he could invest in microfinance banks (his "do-good pocket") in the same way that he invested in real estate projects (his "business pocket"). He started looking for partners and, along with Deutsche Bank and Bankers Trust, soon started a private equity fund to invest in—not make grants to— microfinance banks globally.

Everyone Bob trusted told him this was a mistake: he'd be more valuable to the world if he kept growing Pattillo Properties, because then he'd have more money to give away. But one day, Bob was at church with his then eleven-year-old daughter Kathlyn, making small talk over coffee with other churchgoers after the service. Someone asked Bob, "What do you do for a living?" Bob was about to respond, "Real estate," when tiny Kathlyn chimed in, wagging her finger, saying, "He's in microfinance! He makes loans to women around the world. And they repay!" "My daughter was watching," Bob said, "and she understood what I really cared about."

Within three weeks, he put the wheels in motion to sell his entire company—dedicating 100 percent of his net worth to one-pocket investments. It turned out to be a good financial decision, too—he sold in the mid-2000s, at nearly the height of the real estate bubble. And he realized attractive profits in the microfinance industry—during the Great Recession, the microfinance industry significantly outperformed mainstream private equity and debt.[53] Today microfinance has become a market in the tens of billions.[54]

Bob succeeded because he looked to different places and different people for new ideas. But he didn't stop there. His third big win came once he became interested in ways that technology could bring wealth to the majority of the world, beyond microfinance. He joined forces with Arun Gore, the founding CFO of T-Mobile, to start backing entrepreneurs. Their firm, Gray Ghost Ventures, was the first investor of bKash, the fastest-growing startup in Bangladesh, which has brought more than 10 million Bangladeshis into the formal economy by introducing the idea of sending and saving money over mobile phones, and of M-KOPA Solar, the fastest-growing startup in sub-Saharan Africa, which has brought affordable, renewable solar energy to nearly 1 million homes.

I'm an entrepreneur who got my start thanks to Bob. When I was in my first year at the University of Virginia, my friend and I had an idea for a tech platform that would make civic education more engaging for students across the United States. We had $10,000 in committed sponsorships, but we needed up-front cash to build our website. I didn't know Bob personally, but he and I went to the same church in my hometown of Atlanta. I cold-called his firm, and he suggested we meet at a local dive called Fat Matt's Rib Shack. I think he took the meeting only because he got a kick out of a kid calling him up and asking for money for a startup.

On the back of a sauce-stained sheet he tore out of his notebook, I explained our idea and asked him for a $10,000 grant. He said, "You don't need a grant, but I'd do a $10,000 bridge loan." I said, "That's great! I'll take it! What's a bridge loan?" I was confused: this was an education project, so why not a grant? Bob explained that since I had revenue coming in, if I took an investment—not a grant—we would be in a true partnership.

Anyone who wants to identify the best ideas would do well to live by three traits embodied by Bob Pattillo:

1. He understands that great ideas can come from anywhere, not just New York or Silicon Valley. A white guy investing from Atlanta can learn as much from a woman in rural Bangladesh as he can teach her.

2. He understands that people who have been successful in an industry are often not the best forecasters of new ideas. So he sources ideas from different people, consistently including entrepreneurs and community stakeholders in decision-making.

3. He understands that what's good for society in the long term and what's good for business in the short term do not have to be mutually exclusive. His investments are one-pocket.

Bob is one example of an innovator who has succeeded not by having the best ideas but by seeking out and selecting ideas differently. In the next few chapters, we'll highlight the emerging innovators who are illuminating a path to success beyond the blind spots.

CHAPTER 5

CHANGING THE PROCESS

Why Entrepreneurs Are Better Judges of
New Ideas Than Expert Investors

If I had an hour to solve a problem, I'd spend fifty-five
minutes figuring out the actual problem, and five minutes
on the solution.
  —Albert Einstein

A friend of mine who used to work for a multi-billion-dollar
foundation told me that on her first day, her boss said,
"Congratulations! You'll never have a bad idea again." People
looking for money, he reminded her, typically tell people with
money what they want to hear. Indeed, her biggest challenge
was to constantly seek dissenting information and correct for her
biases—since she represented a big funder, she rarely got negative
feedback directly.

In the past few chapters we've talked about the traditional
venture capital process. The people with capital mostly went to the
same few schools and now live in the same few places, and they're
the ones who get to decide which new ideas see the light of day.
They are inundated with ideas and incentivized to choose a few
big ones that they can quickly flip for profit—with their own biases
always present. Ultimately, there is a power dynamic at play, and
it works to the advantage of the few at the expense of the many.

Bob Pattillo's experience with microfinance offered a window into a different way of thinking. For centuries, banks around the world would not extend credit to low-income people who didn't have a bank account simply because it was too expensive for loan officers to research and process what were, on average, hundred-dollar loans. The "village bank" approach to microfinance changed that dynamic. Instead of loan officers deciding who gets capital, entrepreneurs decide themselves. Billions of dollars have been invested in millions of small-scale entrepreneurs around the world—with a 99 percent repayment rate—because of one big process change: entrepreneurs turned out to be better forecasters of what ideas will be successful.

This insight has been core to the firm that I cofounded, Village Capital. In this chapter I'll tell the story of our investment philosophy, our early years, and insights from our process, which puts decision-making power in the hands of (for-profit) entrepreneurs. I'm not claiming that this is the only solution to venture capital's problems, or even that we've perfected the process ourselves. But I hope to show that it is possible to innovate in the way we support innovation.

MAKERS VERSUS MANAGERS

In his best-selling book *Originals*, Wharton professor Adam Grant describes research done by then-doctoral student Justin Berg on how the circus decides which acts it will perform.[55] In "Balancing on the Creative High-Wire," Berg investigated whether Managers (the ringmasters) or Makers (the circus performers who designed new feats) were more successful at predicting what acts audiences would like.

Berg found that Managers were worse at spotting the best ideas; specifically, they were often poor predictors of which performances would be popular. "Pattern recognition" dictated that they would choose new acts based on what had worked in the past rather than on what audiences would want in the future. Makers were better evaluators of new ideas; they tended to view their peers' ideas not through a lens of "How well does this act resemble what has worked in the past?" but rather "How likely is this to succeed in the future?"

Makers never stop generating new ideas, which helps keep their minds open to novel ways to succeed. The Manager Mindset, on the other hand, encourages the Decision-Maker to sit back and evaluate ideas pitched to them, so they end up doubling down on outdated models of success. Makers are also more likely to respect constructive, honest criticism from fellow Makers, whom they know face the same struggles of going onstage every night and having to make an impression on the audience.

I notice this dynamic every day in the venture capital world. People bet on what they have seen work before, rather than forecast what might work in the future. When someone with a Manager mind-set looks at a new idea, they typically make what I'll call an *assessment*. They evaluate the idea with a series of yes/no questions, and identify all the reasons why it will fail. Is the team fully staffed? Is the idea profitable yet? Have they raised money from anyone else? Does this look like other things that have succeeded? If the answer to these questions is no, the idea is unlikely to go forward. So if you have a great idea but don't fit within anyone's assessment, you're sunk.

A Maker thinks very differently about an idea, making what I'll call a *forecast*. The Maker looks at the idea and thinks of all the reasons why it will succeed. Whereas an assessment is an evaluation against a fixed framework, a forecast evaluates a probability that a certain outcome will happen. Instead of "Do they have the right team?" it's "How likely is it that with the right resources, they can build the right team?" Instead of "Do they have traction?" it's "How likely is it that with the right resources, they can get market traction?"

In his award-winning article "Exploring Intuition and Its Role in Managerial Decision-Making,"[56] Erik Dane of Rice University highlights how experts may actually block the best new ideas by relying on pattern recognition in their decision-making. Experts are great at figuring out how new ideas might fit into existing patterns (assessment), but they often stifle creativity regarding how ideas might work in the future (forecasting).

Some investments are in fact assessment decisions. If I am making a stock market investment or a large private equity investment in a company with years and years of data, I will likely need an in-depth understanding of ingrained patterns—and how companies are fitting them or not. But when I'm investing in a new idea, old patterns don't matter. Kodak famously developed the digital camera internally—then decided it wouldn't work. Microsoft was sure that the iPhone would not get significant market share. The list goes on.

So how can investors eliminate the "pattern recognition" element of investing? We can learn to forecast, rather than assess.

Forecasting is a well-developed technique. The data scientist Philip Tetlock's book *Superforecasters* describes a bold experiment from the US Department of Defense and the CIA. For a decade, thousands of people across the country were asked weekly questions, in exchange for an Amazon gift card, on a range of questions, such as "How likely is it that a self-driving car with a passenger will have an accident by 1 January 2017?" The book *Superforecasters* then looked at the respondents who performed in the top 5 percent overall in terms of the accuracy of their predictions. This small group of everyday people, from schoolteachers to retirees, was able to outperform both the general public and the best experts in the field. Tetlock posits that this was because they didn't have ingrained biases regarding whether certain events would happen.

As one example, the forecasters who predicted that Brexit would happen were twice as likely to predict that Donald Trump would be elected president (an outcome deemed unlikely by pollsters). Forecasters who predicted that Trump would be elected cited "polling error" as the reason, saying, "Polls are not capturing the intent of the US voter correctly" and "Support for Donald Trump is massively underestimated by the polls, just like the polls got the Brexit vote and the Colombian vote on peace accords wrong." They moved beyond a concept introduced by Daniel Kahneman, "What you see is all there is," to look at polls as a variable, not a fixed scorecard for assessment.

One superforecaster summed up the forecaster mind-set by saying that his strategy was "How likely is X to happen?" not "What do I think about X?" This is the approach investors should use when we are choosing which ideas are likely to be successful: forecasting potential rather than assessing progress via pattern recognition.

A FIRST LIGHT FOR NEW IDEAS

Though I now run a venture capital firm, I learned most of what I know from the perspective of a Maker, not a Manager. I've always been an entrepreneur—since before I knew what the word meant.

When I was six, I wanted to grow up to be an inventor. I had a white lab coat and dressed as a mad scientist for Halloween. When I was eight, I set up a "zoo" in my bedroom, put my stuffed animals on exhibit, and tried to charge my family for admission (my mom reminded me when I was writing this book that nobody paid me to attend).

Thanks to Bob Pattillo taking a chance on me, I began working in startups in college, and I haven't looked back. In 2008, in the midst of the Great Recession, Bob offered me a job with the title "Hurricane Chaser." He said he wanted entrepreneurs, not investment bankers, to find the entrepreneurs he'd invest in. His job title was "Inkler" (one who comes up with inklings), and he was proud that he was the first investor in forty-six inklings, but he wanted to do a lot more. He had set aside $10 million of his own money toward First Light, a new fund that could provide inklings around the world with their first shot. First Light's vision was to support 987 new businesses in ten years. (Why 987? As Bob explained, it's the largest three-digit number in the Fibonacci sequence.)

In the first six months, we reviewed nearly a thousand business plans, spoke with nearly two hundred entrepreneurs, and invested in only three companies. What we learned was that in those hundreds of conversations, quantities of business plans didn't translate to quality: most of our meetings with inbound ventures were noise, not signal. A further problem was that we met with entrepreneurs only because of personal connections, or because we had seen them at a conference in San Francisco, or because their startups had won awards. We weren't spreading our net wide enough.

We also learned that we—and most investors—were trying to say no in slow and opaque ways. I saw entrepreneurs playing a guessing game, fishing for the "right answers," rather than having honest conversations about their business. Under the surface, they were asking themselves, "What do we need to do to get investment?" rather than asking us, "What do you think we need to do to be successful as a company?" The power dynamic was not helping the companies, and it was making our jobs as investors difficult. There had to be a better way.

"IF ANGEL INVESTING AND MICROFINANCE HAD A BABY"

In the early days of First Light, Bob would have a regular huddle— he called it the "Bulge"—where our team of eight would evaluate new "inklings" to better spur innovation. At each Bulge meeting, everyone would vote on the ideas, and we'd rank them publicly to see which would bubble to the top.

One consistent winner I kept coming back to: the idea of the "village bank," which I had seen working on the ground in India. In the microfinance industry, Bob and I had seen a structure that worked better in getting capital to people who couldn't otherwise access it. Through a combination of transparency, peer pressure, and interpersonal relationships, villages of Makers demonstrated that they could be trusted to make great investments. The basic inkling was to take the spirit of the "village bank" and apply it to venture capital. The analogy seemed clear.

I worked with Bob, as well as an experienced venture capitalist named Sean Foote, to design the first process. Bob brought his experience from the YPO forum, a peer group of successful young CEOs, and Sean brought his experience as an angel investor in Silicon Valley. We designed a series of pilot programs in which we connected entrepreneurs who were trying to raise capital for their ideas with entrepreneurs who were already working full-time on their ventures. But we added a twist: two founders in the program, chosen by their peers, would each get $100,000 in investment.

We announced the program under the name Village Capital (village banking + venture capital). An early blogger was so intrigued by the peer review concept that he wrote an article describing the model "as if angel investing and microfinance had a baby."[57]

At first, most mainstream investors rejected the idea—one said we were "bonkers." Another told us, "This is going to be worse than *Shark Tank*. They're going to rip each other apart—and these inexperienced entrepreneurs won't even know what they're talking about."

Neither of those things have turned out to be true.

WHAT HAPPENS WHEN WE RELY ON
ENTREPRENEURS TO FORECAST NEW IDEAS?

If you've ever been in a room of your peers, you know who has potential and who doesn't. You know which classmate of yours didn't do the reading and doesn't know his stuff—but manages to say something charismatic when the teacher calls on him. You know which classmate does all her homework but is too shy to speak up. You want to bet on the woman in the front row—but in the systems we have, the guy in the back tends to get the attention of the experts.

A founder's fate is in the hands of a small group of people secretly making decisions based on their unconscious biases. These biases will never disappear, but transparency calls them out. In our early pilots with Village Capital, the process was extremely unstructured—and done by secret ballot. We had each founder rank their peers in order, with no fixed criteria. Sometimes, it worked out great. Other times, it was a popularity contest ("I just love Sam!") or a "sympathy vote" ("Greg, bless her heart, has worked so hard on this. If we don't invest in her, no one else will."). Over time, we have retooled the process to make it structured and transparent. Teams evaluate one another on two criteria: potential and return on investment. If I rank you well or poorly, the entire peer group can see the results.

My colleagues at First Light worked incredibly hard to implement an array of pilots in different places: New Orleans, Boulder, Mumbai, and San Francisco. The peer review methodology is not something we invented. In addition to microfinance's "village bank" concept, academia has utilized peer review for centuries. Immigrants often use a form of peer review to make "handshake loans," generating startup capital for a new hardware store, gas station, or motel. Silicon Valley venture capital firms often employ entrepreneurs for sourcing and diligence. Makers have long played a role in the forecasting of new ideas—we just don't always notice.

If we are open and transparent about the biases that influence our decisions, we'll improve the diversity of ideas that get a shot—and the results of our investment. .

A BOTTOM-UP PROCESS CAN YIELD BETTER RESULTS THAN A TOP-DOWN PROCESS

Peer selection has always been somewhat disruptive to the venture capital industry. Many still make the argument that entrepreneurs don't have the training, experience, or expertise necessary to reliably identify the most promising innovations that are ready for investment, nor do they know how to accurately assess the value of one another's companies.

This criticism, I think, is true for assessment decisions. Later-stage venture capital and private equity investors deploying tens of millions of dollars in growth capital have years of evidence of a company's performance and are able to make decisions based on assessing a company's growth trajectory. But investing in new ideas is a forecasting decision, and we have substantial evidence that entrepreneurs are better at predicting whether an idea and its early execution will be successful.

When evaluating new ideas, we need to get past the idea that entrepreneurs and investors are on opposite sides of the table. Many venture investors tout their firms as "founder-friendly" or "founder-first." We can't think of a more deliberate way to show we're founder-first than to actually give founders the power to determine how we invest.

Peer selection isn't a silver bullet to eliminate innovation blind spots, but it's one framework that has evidence of working. For one thing, the cost of making smaller investments is lower, since managers don't have to do diligence on hundreds of companies.

Instead, entrepreneurs—who already have the market and sector context—can conduct in-depth analysis of one another's businesses, building relationships along the way. Peer selection can also help scale investments to different locations—if your capital is in New York or San Francisco but you want to invest in, say, Des Moines or Nashville.

Of course, diversifying your investments alone won't guarantee better results. A team without the capital, network, and resources to execute will still fall flat—and one that doesn't understand the market they're operating in will struggle to make money for investors. But investors who build a process that considers a broader range of ideas will be more likely to succeed.

We've seen how investing differently can, in many ways, create a more valuable portfolio. Less than 5 percent of venture funding goes to women founders. Women entrepreneurs struggle not because they are less successful, but because of the cognitive biases that we've laid out in prior chapters. Our first board chair at Village Capital, Joy Anderson, and Jackie VanderBrug, now a leader at Bank of America, pioneered the field of "gender lens investing," highlighting how cognitive biases often skew toward male-run companies and encourage people to change business structures in order to more intentionally value the role women can play on boards, leadership teams, and in the workforce.

Peer selection is one way to more appropriately value women founders. Consider the example of Emily Morris, a brilliant engineer from Georgia Tech in Atlanta. Her company, Emrgy, is essentially a floating pontoon that can be placed in any moving body of water to generate hydroelectric power. Despite a contract with the City of Atlanta, more traction than most energy companies, and a major Department of Energy pilot, Emily struggled to raise funding. She failed to win business plan competitions, even though she knew her product was better than what the other people were pitching. A local angel group expressed interest, but over the diligence process, Emily realized no one was taking the time to get to know her business.

We at Village Capital were Emily's first investor. She went through a program we operated that focused on water technology, and she won the peer rank in a runaway. Why did she succeed in peer review? She said that the process was much more collaborative and productive, and ultimately gave her a much fairer shot than the traditional venture process. Her ability to be honest was rewarded: she didn't feel as though she had any incentive—as she had in *Shark Tank*–style investor pitches—to promise the moon.

Village Capital's women entrepreneurs dramatically overperform in the peer selection process. Just 25 percent of our participating entrepreneurs have had women cofounders, yet women have received investment nearly 40 percent of the time. Our women founders point to the open and collaborative nature of the process of peer selection, which rewards those who work well with one another.

We've measured performance over time in the companies with women cofounders who received a seed investment from Village Capital. We found that by controlling for similar industries and geographies, female-run companies outperform male-led firms by at least 20 percent in revenue earned and full- and part-time jobs created, yet still attract only 80 percent as much equity funding as male-run companies. Yet when firms with women cofounders receive a first investment in their first two years of operation, we found that their revenue growth exceeds male-run companies even more—30 percent—and the entire fundraising gap is closed.

WE NEED TO INNOVATE IN THE *WAY* WE INVEST, NOT JUST WHAT WE INVEST IN

I don't think that peer selection and expert selection are the only options in the venture capital process. I'm always excited to hear of other innovations that make fundraising more transparent and level the playing field for founders.

Take, for example, crowdfunding. In 2002, Danae Ringelmann was working on Wall Street at J. P. Morgan, but her real passion was theater. She wanted to raise money to produce a play, but theater didn't fit into anyone's "pattern." She started asking around for advice and realized that the fundraising process didn't work for most people.

She and two other friends from business school started Indiegogo, a platform allowing anyone to "crowdfund" a play, a startup company, a community art project, or any other venture. Platforms like Indiegogo, Kickstarter, and others have helped thousands of entrepreneurs raise money they would otherwise not have been able to. On these websites, you can post an idea for a product or service, then request money straight from interested buyers. This democratized process has produced noteworthy results: 5 percent of people receiving financing from venture capitalists are women, whereas 50 percent of people raising money through crowdfunding campaigns are women.

Other innovators are looking to break down the "warm introduction." Arlan Hamilton is an African-American woman who, as an entrepreneur, realized quickly that if you don't already know someone with money, it's tough to get funding in the venture capital world. She launched a firm, Backstage Capital, to help founders from underrepresented backgrounds get "backstage." One of her most unusual and impressive metrics of success is the percentage of founders who cold e-mail the firm and eventually get funding: 30 percent of her investments have come not from a warm introduction, but from a cold call. She's getting first crack at many ideas that other venture firms never even see.

Whether it's changing the funding process or encouraging a different pipeline, innovations around who gets a chance to access capital yield better outcomes.

VILLAGE CAPITAL: EARLY DAYS AND PROMISING RESULTS

I launched Village Capital with a loan from Bob Pattillo in 2009, and a pre-commitment of capital to entrepreneurs through a few initial pilots. We decided to start in New Orleans. The night before our first pilot program, Bob and I were having a beer on Magazine Street and listening to jazz. "What if it fails?" we asked each other. We eventually realized that failing would not be any worse than the current, broken way we were doing things. The more important question was "But what if it succeeds?" We could create a vision of a different world.

After promising signs from early pilots, including New Orleans, we decided to launch our own fund. I met and joined forces with Victoria Fram, who had investment expertise that I didn't. She became a cofounder in charge of managing our investment fund, whose initial investments are made 100 percent through peer selection.

We're seeing vastly different results than what the traditional venture capital process produces. As mentioned earlier, 78 percent of startup investment in traditional venture capital in the United States (and 50 percent worldwide) goes to California, Massachusetts, and New York. In our portfolio, only 10 percent of the companies are from those three states. In traditional venture capital, less than 10 percent of startup investment goes to women and less than 1 percent to people of color. In our portfolio, 40 percent of the companies have a female founder or cofounder, and 20 percent of the founders are people of color.

From day one we've taken a one-pocket approach by addressing two existential threats for society. First, we're investing in companies that create economic opportunity for people, regardless of background. This includes sectors such as:

- Financial health: One in three people in the United States don't have a bank account, and 50 percent of Americans can't access $400 in an emergency.
- Education: By 2020, two-thirds of jobs in the United States will require some amount of post-secondary training or certification. Today, only one in three Americans have reached this.
- Healthcare: 20 percent of the US GDP is spent on healthcare, and the population is rapidly aging.

We're also investing in sectors that improve the resource sustainability of the planet, including:

- Energy: In 2016, renewable energy became cheaper—and created more new jobs—than fossil fuels. By 2050, energy sources are expected to be 80 percent renewable.
- Agriculture: We will need to produce as much food in the next forty years as we have in the last eight thousand years to feed a projected global population of ten billion people.

We're still in the early days, but the results we've seen so far are promising. In mainstream entrepreneurship, 50 percent of businesses fail in five years, but 90 percent of our companies are still surviving and growing seven years in. Our companies are growing 200 percent year-on-year in revenue, and we've seen other investors put another $200 million into these entrepreneurs' efforts to solve real-world problems.

In doing so, we've embraced the maxim "It's not who you know; it's who you get to know," allowing us to meet thousands of innovators who would otherwise remain in our blind spot. In the next chapter, we'll talk about how to do this, exemplified by an Illuminator named Steve Case, a cross-country bus tour, and a call to action: the Rise of the Rest.

CHAPTER 6

BUILDING THE PIPELINE

If you happen to be a star running back in West Texas or
California, the whole country knows who you are from
the time you are in middle school. And we create an
environment for you to go to Southern Cal and then to be a
Green Bay Packer. Everybody expects you to do something
great. Have you ever heard of someone telling a middle-
schooler they expect them to be a great entrepreneur?
—Jim Clifton, CEO, Gallup

In America, we spend billions of dollars making sure that high
school and college athletes have their shot at the American
Dream. As Jim Clifton noted, no matter your zip code or who you
are, if you've got the potential to be a superstar athlete, you'll be
on the radar of great college coaches by the time you're in middle
school. Whether you're in inner-city Baltimore or rural Nebraska,
the billion-dollar talent pipeline created by universities, pro sports
leagues, and shoe companies will ensure you've got a shot at a
lucrative career.

Setting aside the larger issues around college athletics and academics, the college athlete recruiting pipeline gives me confidence
that we can close blind spots around entrepreneurship. The billion-
dollar pipeline for athletes didn't come from nowhere; it had to be
created. And we can create a pipeline for entrepreneurs, too.

One of my heroes and inspirations is my grandfather, Vic
Bubas, who helped create that college athlete pipeline. He was
born to Croatian immigrants in working-class Gary, Indiana,

where he grew up working in the family's hardware store. He earned a scholarship to North Carolina State, where as a point guard he took the basketball team to the Final Four under legendary coach Everett Case. He served as an assistant to Coach Case until Duke University, which at that time had one of the weaker basketball teams in the country, offered him the head coaching job in 1959.

Stalking the sidelines of Duke's Cameron Indoor Stadium, my grandfather couldn't help noticing that college coaches tended to recruit players from their own backyards. This was one of the reasons for Duke's basketball struggles: my grandfather had to recruit head-to-head with national powerhouses (and much larger schools) like the University of North Carolina and NC State. But my grandfather believed that there were great ballplayers everywhere—whether they were immigrant kids like himself in Gary, Indiana, or inner-city ballplayers in Philadelphia.

To get ahead, my grandfather needed to innovate. He was one of the first college coaches to begin tracking high school recruits across the country, starting in their freshman year. He was the first coach to have a video machine in his office, watching tapes of players from all over. He was especially interested in kids from far-flung areas who were overlooked by other coaches.

"Vic taught us all how to recruit," said Dean Smith, the Hall of Fame basketball coach of UNC. "For a while, all of us were trying to catch up with him." My grandfather was also one of the first coaches in the South to recruit African-Americans. One of Duke's first All-Americans, Mike Lewis, was from Missoula, Montana; his father was shocked when the head coach of Duke University showed up at their door.

My grandfather's recruits delivered success—he took his team to the Final Four, the pinnacle of success, three times in ten years. In 2007, he was inducted into the National Collegiate Basketball

Hall of Fame, where his biography says he was "widely credited with pioneering the art of recruiting college basketball players."

If we take a page from Coach Bubas and change the way we recruit for entrepreneurs, talented kids anywhere can have a shot at success in business—and open untapped markets for the people who support them.

THE RISE OF THE REST

Most investors today are investing in what and who they know. They're recruiting the way UNC and NC State did in the early 1960s: meeting the kids they know and understand. Who's thinking differently?

In the mid-1980s, a young entrepreneur and marketing whiz named Steve Case drove thousands of miles across the country looking for the best pizza that America had to offer. Steve had a young college graduate's dream job title—Head of Pizza Development for Pizza Hut—and a dream job: to travel the country in search of the best pizza anywhere and send it back to the mothership. While traveling across America, he would play at night from his hotel room with an early version of the Internet, and he knew it was the future.

Steve's brother, Dan, an investment banker who had been working with early technology pioneers, introduced Steve to two DC-based techies, Bill von Meister and Jim Kimsey, who had an interesting idea to get people online. The meeting led to the creation of America Online in 1985, which became the most valuable startup of the 1990s.

AOL was in Virginia, not New York or Silicon Valley, because its headquarters literally sat on top of the fastest Internet in the world. In the 1980s and 1990s, the early adopters of the Internet created two main connectivity points, or Metropolitan Area Exchanges:

MAE-East, near Dulles Airport in Virginia, and MAE-West (no relationship to the actress) in Silicon Valley. AOL, MCI, and other early Internet-focused companies set up their headquarters near Dulles so they could tap into MAE-East, the fastest Internet connectivity in the country. The Internet in its early days required a series of underground cables to transmit signals, and the interchanges were critical for speed. If you were transmitting a packet of information from Chicago to Miami in 1991, for example, your signal had to "change tracks" in Dulles, much like a train.

Washington was also a helpful location because the Internet faced policy barriers. Until 1990, consumers couldn't legally access the Internet; only 3 percent of Americans had ever been online. America Online needed to educate government regulators as much as it needed to educate the public. Steve even struggled to explain to his parents what the Internet was—almost ten years after he started AOL, they were still asking when he was going to get a real job.

AOL wasn't the only entity to try to solve this problem. AOL had a range of competitors: AT&T launched Prodigy. Boston-based CompuServe was actually the first company to offer Internet to consumers. And General Electric—where a marketing upstart named Jean Villanueva was on a team trying to drive disruptive innovation within a big company—created the GEnie.

Steve recognized that the company that would win the race to get America online would be the company that made the Internet easiest to use. If your friends and family could all get online, you'd be more likely to use it; as the team often said in the early days of AOL, the "killer app"—why people will use the Internet—would be community.

AOL beat its competitors by being easier to use and understand, and making the Internet itself easy to use and understand. The company succeeded because they helped everyday Americans become aware of what the Internet could do.

Meanwhile, Jean Villanueva left GE to become director of marketing at AOL. (She and Steve later married; today, Jean Case is CEO of the Case Foundation and the first female chairman of the National Geographic Society.) Today, you might remember AOL best for the CDs you received in the mail—the indiscriminate flooding of Americans' mailboxes was a wildly successful, fearlessly aggressive marketing campaign that served to help people understand what the Internet was. Jean, Steve, and the rest of the AOL team also developed a cross-country bus tour to celebrate and popularize the Internet. AOL won America's attention and became the most valuable Internet company of the 1990s.

When Steve Case first built AOL in Washington, DC, people thought it was just a government town. But the company's success transformed the DC area, and Steve has ever since been on a one-pocket mission to support entrepreneurs across the country. He calls this movement the "Rise of the Rest."

ON THE ROAD

In the summer of 2014, Steve Case and his investment firm, Revolution, again fired up a bus for a new tour. Whereas the bus tour in the 1990s educated America about the Internet, this time the goal would be to seek out entrepreneurs across the country. In partnership with Village Capital, Rise of the Rest has now brought its bus tour to twenty-five cities, investing at least $100,000 per city as seed capital in local startups. In Rise of the Rest cities, investors can see higher returns, entrepreneurs can have significantly lower costs, and consumers can get great products at a better value for their money.

For example, in 2015, Revolution invested in a company, Shinola, whose founders Steve and Revolution met on the bus tour in Detroit. Shinola creates beautiful, high-quality bicycles, watches, and other goods, while employing over five hundred people in manufacturing jobs in downtown Detroit. Shinola is creating a vision of what good jobs can look like in communities that fall on hard times. CEO Steve Bock argued in the *Washington Post* that Shinola could exist only in Detroit. "People keep telling us," said Bock, "how much Shinola has done for Detroit. But it's the absolute opposite: it's what Detroit has done for Shinola."[58]

Detroit provides a cautionary tale for the "pattern recognition" mind-set in place today—and hope for other communities. Fifty years ago, Detroit was the wealthiest US city per capita.[59] It was the Silicon Valley of the mid-twentieth century (Silicon Valley itself was filled with apple orchards). Detroit rose because its city leaders innovated, betting on the automobile. Many factors changed Detroit's leadership position, including globalization, but it was Detroit's inability to innovate that led it to eventual bankruptcy. Today, thanks to firms like Shinola, Detroit is telling a more optimistic story, one we'll explore more deeply in chapter 13.

Silicon Valley is today the most forward-thinking, active supporter of new ideas, but we're seeing increasing evidence that other cities are rising. A 2015 *Harvard Business Review* study illustrated how, while the Midwest is still tracking well below the coasts, the region saw more companies funded in 2014 than at any point in the past. And the talented people in Silicon Valley are starting to go elsewhere. A slew of startups and now venture funds have recently left Silicon Valley for LA (Snapchat), Chicago (Keepsake), Seattle (Sherbert), and even Columbus, Ohio (Drive Capital).

The re-shuffling of the world's talent is only beginning. Most of my friends in Silicon Valley moved there when they were single; now that they have kids, they're searching for opportunities from Colorado to Oklahoma to Tennessee. In 2015, 50 percent of the people leaving the Bay Area were millennials. As Adam Wiener, Redfin's chief growth officer, announced to other executives in early 2016, predicting a rush of talent away from the Valley: "The dam has broken."[60] Four regions in the United States are already seeing a higher per capita unicorn success rate than Silicon Valley, with Salt Lake-Provo, Utah, in the lead.[61]

Fifty percent of the *Fortune* 500 in 2000 were no longer on the list fifteen years later, which suggests that we're going to see many new *Fortune* 500 companies in the next twenty years that are just starting up now. And since 86 percent of the *Fortune* 500 are now based outside New York, Boston, and San Francisco, odds are very good that these new companies will be located elsewhere as well.

CITIES SHOULD USE THEIR COMPETITIVE ADVANTAGE RATHER THAN TRY TO CLONE SILICON VALLEY

Cities everywhere want to become the launching pad for the next tech sensation: the next Facebook, Twitter, WhatsApp, or other multi-billion-dollar winner. Wherever I travel—whether to Lagos, Nigeria; Mumbai, India; or Raleigh, North Carolina—I hear the same question: "How can we recreate Silicon Valley here?" The better question would be "What can we do better than Silicon Valley in the future economy?"

Rise of the Rest is set to succeed in a one-pocket world—but only if cities embrace what makes them great, rather than make themselves a Procrustean bed in an effort to copy Silicon Valley. Reflecting on the creation and growth of the Internet, Steve Case wrote a book, *The Third Wave*, inspired by Alvin Toffler's book of the same name in which he predicted the spread of the information revolution (following the "waves" of the agricultural and industrial revolutions).

In Case's book, the first wave of the Internet—which AOL and its peers led—accomplished getting people on the Internet. The second wave, dominated by Silicon Valley, helped people communicate with one another using the Internet infrastructure. But as the Internet becomes more pervasive, Case argues that a third wave of startups will dominate how the Internet improves every-day life—from food to health to education to energy to transportation. And startups will lead the way, no matter where they are located—so long as they target the industries ripe for disruption.

We see these disruptions everywhere. On the first Rise of the Rest tour, the bus visited Nashville, where you'll find a bunch of offshoots of Hospital Corporation of America, the country's largest hospital management company, which Dr. Thomas Frist (father of former Senate majority leader Dr. Bill Frist) founded in 1968. The HCA ecosystem is yielding startups such as Aspire Health, which is helping solve urgent challenges around end-of-life care by giving families the information they need to make difficult decisions on where to do rehabilitation and what procedures should be done. And even though Aspire started as a local Nashville startup, when these companies succeed, Silicon Valley pays attention. Aspire's largest investor is now the venture arm of Silicon Valley titan Google.

When we invest in ideas from unexpected places, we can close many of the blind spots we have. Take one of my favorite examples: Pear Deck. Our education system, like our venture capital system, favors the people who play the game the best. The kid who knows exactly what to say to the teacher, and whose parents know how to coach them to success, gets the advantages. The kid who is afraid to raise her hand, even if she does all the reading and sits in the front row every day, gets overlooked.

Pear Deck, a homegrown technology crafted by a Quaker wife-and-husband team in Iowa City, is solving this problem. Riley and Michael Eynon-Lynch took their inspiration from the Quaker town meeting, where people speak their mind when they are so moved and comfortably engage with the community on their own terms. They applied this thinking to the classroom. When a teacher is flying through lessons, asking questions and provoking answers, Pear Deck's technology gives kids the opportunity to think through and voice their opinions in whatever way that they are most comfortable and confident, whether it's drawing a response or answering a multiple-choice question. Village Capital and Revolution coinvested in Pear Deck, and we've seen classrooms give teachers a standing ovation at the end of a lesson, with the student discussions more resembling a symphony than a rote call-and-response. In its first year, half a million students were developing their ideas every day on the Pear Deck platform.

Pear Deck's Iowa City location surprises most people I talk to. But if you took the Iowa Test of Basic Skills as an elementary student, you'll know that Iowa knows how to give tests. Iowa City is the home of the ACT, taken by millions of students yearly, and its largest nonpublic employer is Pearson, the world's biggest education company. If you want to learn how to evaluate and improve learning outcomes, there may well be no better place than Iowa City, which gives an education sector company that operates there a unique advantage. Perhaps thanks in part to this advantage, Pear Deck has broken into the mainstream: they're now one of the most-used Google applications in education.

If we want to improve the dynamism of our economy, we need more companies like Pear Deck and Shinola, not more Instagrams.

CHAPTER 7

ONE-POCKET THINKING

Why Do We Know What Things Cost
but Not What They're Worth?

Something is profoundly wrong with the way we live today.
For thirty years we have made a virtue out of the pursuit
of material self-interest: indeed, this very pursuit now
constitutes whatever remains of our sense of collective
purpose. We know what things cost but have no idea what
they are worth. We no longer ask of a judicial ruling or a
legislative act: Is it good? Is it fair? Is it just? Is it right? Will
it help bring about a better society or a better world? Those
used to be the political questions, even if they invited no
easy answers. We must learn once again to pose them.
  —Tony Judt, *Ill Fares the Land*

It is not down on any map; true places never are.
  —Herman Melville, *Moby Dick; or, The Whale*

In 2008, if you wanted to learn the direction the world was going
in education, you'd go to the bar of the Taj Banjara hotel in
Hyderabad, India. Most nights, you'd meet an iconoclastic British
professor of education studies, James Tooley, nursing a gin and
tonic. In June 2008, I had just joined the Indian School Finance
Company (ISFC), a startup in Hyderabad, and to learn the lay of
the land, I joined Professor Tooley for a drink.

A tall, bespectacled Brit with a rumpled jacket, James told me about his expertise: low-cost private schools in emerging markets. As a professor studying international education, he was surprised in a 2000 visit to Hyderabad to learn that most low-income kids went not to public schools run by the government, as they would in the West, but to low-cost private schools. These educational institutions, often set up in a storefront shop, cost between $2 and $10 a month—which, while it seems like a tiny amount, is up to 30 percent of the income of the families who send their kids to these schools. Professor Tooley had learned that similar types of schools also educated a majority of the poor in Nigeria, Indonesia, and dozens of other countries around the world. In Hyderabad alone, over three thousand small schools were trying to deliver a better education from the bottom up.

ISFC was essentially a microfinance bank that made small infrastructure loans to these private schools to make improvements, such as computer labs and additional classrooms. But most of these schools weren't on a map. To get in the system and be registered, school owners often had to pay substantial bribes: Professor Tooley and a colleague, Pauline Dixon, did a study that showed that a principal's willingness to pay a bribe was a greater predictor of whether a school was "recognized" by the government than the students' test scores.

My job was to walk door to door and ask these schools whether they wanted a loan to make improvements and, if so, what they would do with them. I carried with me a map of Hyderabad and rode shotgun on the scooter of my colleague, Pushpraj. We'd go through alleyways of just-built ramshackle neighborhoods in the shadow of HITEC City, where thousands of migrants from rural India had just relocated. When I saw a building that looked like a school, I'd go in and ask to speak to the principal.

On one of my first visits, I interviewed an exceptional leader named Preetha, who had formerly owned a chain of kirana shops—

essentially convenience stores. She noticed that thousands of families had moved to Hyderabad, and there weren't enough schools to accommodate them. Her first school was in an old storefront where she used to run a convenience store, and she had designs to expand to two more.

When I explained what my company did, she asked for a loan to build separate boys' and girls' restrooms. She explained that a major contributor to whether girls stay in school is if there are separate bathrooms; when girls reach a certain age, their parents often pull them out of school if the bathrooms aren't segregated.[62] Preetha said, "I want to educate these girls, and at the same time, when they drop out, I'm losing half my customer base. It's killing my margins!" Preetha wanted to invest in girls' bathrooms as a one-pocket investment, and her school was one of our company's first loans.

In many places, low-cost private schools are the only option. In fast-growing megacities such as Hyderabad, India, or Lagos, Nigeria, some slum areas do not have a government-run public school within miles, but there's a private school on nearly every corner. And these schools deliver better outcomes. The best assessments we have demonstrate that students at private schools are outperforming the status quo—most notably in English, which in India is the best predictor of employability—at one-third the cost of service delivery.

HOW ONE-POCKET THINKING IS BECOMING THE STATUS QUO

How did my career evolve such that I found myself walking door to door in the slums of Hyderabad, asking principals if they wanted loans?

I spent a lot of my time as an undergraduate at the University of Virginia pursuing the startup I told you about earlier and other out-of-the-box ideas. After graduation, I was fortunate enough to win a Marshall Scholarship: two years at the University of Oxford. The Marshall Scholarship was a first-rate experience, but if I'm honest, the main reason I applied was that it was the "default option" for my career—it was a prestigious, fully-funded merit scholarship that seemed like the best next step.

At Oxford, the "default options" kept coming in front of my peers and me. Every week, consulting firms such as McKinsey and investment banks such as Goldman Sachs hosted recruiting events for the Marshall and Rhodes Scholars. I almost took one of these jobs, and I don't blame my peers who did: they paid well, and going to these firms was easy and seamless.

Instead, I asked a broad range of people for advice, including Bob Pattillo. Bob connected me with ISFC's CEO, David Kyle, who had spent his career in investment banking with Citigroup. But on September 11, 2001, David was sitting in his office at Citi's head-quarters in New York when he saw two planes slam into the World Trade Center across the street. He quit his job within a few months.

Reflecting on his twenty-year banking career, David says, "My job was literally to make billionaires as much money as possible." Over the course of his second career, he instead became interested in how finance could improve education. He met Bob, and they launched the "inkling" that became the Indian School Finance Company. In the midst of a patchy Skype call, David told me, "We've got a lot to do here in India. Come help out."

Instead of a formal job description and a signing bonus from a firm whose name you'd recognize, I was promised a paycheck of $1,000 per month (still very significant purchasing power in India!) in a city I'd never heard of. My job description was "Come help out."

Today, the Indian School Finance Company has over $50 million under management and is making loans to low-cost private schools in over a dozen cities across India. Two colleagues of mine on the early ISFC team have launched a spin-off in Bangalore, called Varthana, that is expanding the market, and Village Capital has invested in a third, Shiksha Finance, in Chennai. Bridge International Academies in East Africa has attracted investment from the likes of Bill Gates, Mark Zuckerberg, Pearson, and more.

The idea of investing in low-cost private schools in 2008 was an "inkling"; today, it's an industry. And it all happened because smart investors, senior leaders, and young professionals are increasingly becoming one-pocket thinkers. Bob, as an investor, seeded ISFC because he was done with two-pocket investing. David, as a CEO, had quit a two-pocket career to launch a one-pocket firm. And I, as an employee joining the workforce, wanted a one-pocket career.

Broader societal trends back up what I'm seeing at a ground level: 69 percent of millennials value the impact of their investments over their financial returns.[63] Careers that represent one-pocket thinking, such as social entrepreneurship and impact investing (we'll discuss both further, below), are now top-five career choices for students from the best business schools.[64] And 90 percent of millennials say it's important that their job has a purpose beyond just a paycheck.[65]

Why, then, do most companies, foundations, and people still subscribe to two-pocket thinking?

HOW DID WE GET TO TWO-POCKET THINKING?

Berkshire Hathaway founder Warren Buffett, the most successful investor of the past thirty years, once said that socially responsible investing wouldn't be successful because "no one can serve two masters"—that is, both money and social good. I've heard this quoted numerous times as a defense of two-pocket thinking, but I've always thought it was being used in a misleading way. I recognize the quote about serving two masters from the Bible; the rest of the verse says, "You cannot serve both God and money," which is a different message entirely. From my own faith background, I take this charge seriously. When you look at the original intent of the line, it's in fact a devastating critique of two-pocket thinking. If you can't serve both God and money, then it should be impossible to separate the two in different pockets when you're building a career.

Buffett and other two-pocket thinkers are making two arguments. First, they're arguing that nonprofits are better than companies at addressing social problems. Second, they're arguing that companies without a social mission are better than mission-driven companies at making money.

I believe these are both myths. Even if the first argument were true—if nonprofits were better at solving the world's biggest problems—we would still run into another problem: the philanthropic sector is so small that even the most effective philanthropy in the world wouldn't solve systemic problems. But the second argument is problematic, too. There is growing evidence—from customers, founders, employees, and investors—that it pays off, on the bottom line, to have a long-term mission that matters.

How did we develop two-pocket thinking? Historically, philanthropy has been community-based. Henry Ford set up his first foundation to solve problems in his own backyard. He funded schools in Detroit, Dearborn, and other communities in Michigan because he knew that the students who graduated would likely work for him. If students didn't have access to a good education, his community and his bottom line would both suffer.

But in the early twentieth century, entrepreneurs such as John D. Rockefeller and Andrew Carnegie developed the concept of a modern foundation to solve whatever social problems they found important. American foundations now regularly give away over $50 billion a year, and the world of philanthropy has done wonderful things. But in some ways, philanthropy has also become a one-size-fits-all solution to complicated problems. The foundation and nonprofit world are subservient to the capital markets. Foundations are, by law, required to dedicate only 5 percent of their assets to their charitable purpose. And just as in the venture capital industry, when foundations face an onslaught of ideas and limited time, they are likely to make grants to people and companies and causes they already know and understand. Peter Buffett, Warren's son, once described the in-group bias of the philanthropic world as the "charitable industrial complex."

The philanthropic sector is often just as isolating and closed as the for-profit sector, with similarly destructive power dynamics: grant makers are too often disconnected from the problem at hand, so innovators often end up building what funders want to support rather than what the world demands. It is a top-down model that is often unresponsive to the true needs of the people on the receiving end of the foundation's work.

The nonprofit sector isn't ineffective; we just expect too much from it when it's such a small part of our entire financial system. In the United States, companies have created a world where workers don't have quality healthcare benefits or retirement security, and we expect the incredibly expensive social safety net of the government to pick up the tab. In many emerging markets, we see multinational companies that do not pay workers enough for basic living conditions, and we expect international development agencies and nonprofits to fill the gaps.

But I'm seeing an encouraging trend of pushback to the old "grant" pocket and "investment" pocket way of thinking: a new wave of one-pocket thinkers are illuminating blind spots between pure philanthropy and the capital markets.

THE RISE OF IMPACT INVESTING

In 2007, Antony Bugg-Levine, a program officer at the Rockefeller Foundation, convened a global group of practitioners at John D.

Rockefeller's old villa at Lake Como, Italy, to give one-pocket think-ing a market presence. A movement was brewing, and Antony wanted to give it a name. After tossing around various phrases—"social venture capital," "social entrepreneurship," "triple-bottom-line business"—the group agreed upon "impact investing."

If you want to understand how the impact investing movement has grown, there are several great books on the subject. Antony and Jed Emerson, who pioneered the term "blended value" and was one of the early "one-pocket thinkers," coauthored a book called *Impact Investing*. Judith Rodin, CEO of the Rockefeller Foundation, provided much of the early funding for the movement; her book is called *The Power of Impact Investing*. A third book, *Collaborative Capitalism and the Rise of Impact Investing*, by Cathy Clark, Jed Emerson, and Ben Thornley, tells more of the background story, which is an often surprising clash of cultures: the early market-ing of the idea of impact investing may have taken place among a handful of heavy-hitters at a lakeside villa, but the idea took on a life of its own over the next several decades thanks to a collabora-tion of strange and wonderful innovators.

So how did these ideas all come together? We have to go back to the 1970s, when small groups of innovators around the world began to develop one-pocket investment structures. We've already met Bangladeshi professor Muhammad Yunus, who, in 1976, launched a research project to see how women running small businesses in rural areas could access capital. His "inkling" became the Grameen Bank, and earned Yunus a Nobel Peace Prize. Hundreds of microfinance banks around the world eventu-ally copied Grameen's "village banking" model.

Also in 1976, an enterprising Washington lawyer named Wayne Silby launched an investment group to securitize Small Business Administration loans, which helped the financial mar-kets back businesses in underserved communities, bringing capi-tal to blind spots. In the 1980s, a series of unusual collaborators helped Silby take his out-of-the-box ideas mainstream. First was Josh Mailman, the scion of a wealthy New York family, who had founded a group called the Doughnuts (in his words, "nuts with dough"). These wealthy young heirs and heiresses wanted to do something more with their money than live the New York high life. Wayne and Josh, along with other collaborators, made initial investments in one-pocket companies such as Stonyfield Farm, one of the first organic yogurt companies; Seventh Generation, one of the first companies to manufacture environmentally friendly cleaning products; and ice cream maker Ben & Jerry's, a pioneer in sustainability and fair trade.

Wayne also joined forces with an entrepreneur named Shari Berenbach to launch the Calvert Foundation. Calvert developed the idea of raising money from retail investors and investing in low-income but fast-developing parts of cities. Calvert, and many of the investors it inspired, financed much of the regeneration of America's cities that you can see today in places like Cincinnati's Over-the-Rhine district and the 14th Street Corridor in Washington, DC.

By the 1990s, the disparate "impact investing" groups around the world were beginning to come together in a formal capital markets structure. Entrepreneurs Maria Otero and Michael Chu turned community development nonprofit Accion into a firm that would invest heavily in microfinance in Latin America in the same way that the Grameen Bank and its early partners were investing in South Asia. In the United States, formal investor groups such as Investors' Circle and Social Venture Network began to pool their resources and formally make one-pocket investments.

In the 2000s, commercial wins began to materialize. Unilever acquired Ben & Jerry's, making Unilever the largest fair-trade product sourcer in the world—and increasing the income of farmers globally by millions.[66] Compartamos Banco, an early Accion investee, went public and made investors returns any venture capitalist would be excited about. SKS Microfinance, launched by Muhammad Yunus disciple Vikram Akula, became the fastest-growing startup in India, raising commercial investment from Silicon Valley titans such as Sequoia Capital and Vinod Khosla. SKS ultimately went public on the Bombay Stock Exchange, at returns of over 200 percent to investors.

And the capital markets began to coalesce. Bob Pattillo was an early board member of Accion and launched the first private equity fund in microfinance banks. Another group, Unitus Labs, helped accelerate the microfinance industry by providing capital and management expertise to fledgling bank managers. Early Unitus board members and investors included Bob Gay, cofounder of Bain Capital; Joseph Grenny, a successful entrepreneur; Mike Murray, an early Apple marketing chief (famous for creating the "1984" TV ad); and Jim Sorenson of Sorenson Communications, whom we met in chapter 4.

In the late 2000s, around the time that Antony Bugg-Levine convened the impact investing summit, it was clear that a movement was emerging. Unitus launched Elevar, an equity firm, to make investments in banks. As of the end of 2013, Elevar's fund had made 21 percent in total return to private investors—a return that any private equity or venture capital fund would be happy to deliver. Accion spun off its own fund, Quona, and raised $141 million from the private sector. And while impact investing didn't begin in Silicon Valley, it spread there: Nancy Pfund, a J. P. Morgan investor, spun off a Bay Area group called DBL (Double Bottom-Line) Partners, which became early investors in companies such as Tesla. And San Francisco's SOCAP, the Social Capital Markets, began holding an annual conference "at the intersection of money and meaning" that now draws more than ten thousand attendees.

In the last decade, each of the top fourteen investment banks has established an "impact investing" or "social finance" practice.[67] When former Massachusetts governor Deval Patrick left office in

2015, he chose to run a new one-pocket impact investing unit for Bain Capital.[68] Pope Francis has encouraged impact investing for the church's endowments—a one-pocket strategy incorporating 100 percent of church assets, not just the usual 5 percent.[69] And global private equity pioneer TPG launched the $2 billion Rise Fund, managed by Maya Chorengel, cofounder of Elevar. It is one of the largest impact investment firms of its type, with investments from global celebrities such as Bono and Richard Branson.

ONE-POCKET INVESTING ISN'T EASY

Impact investing hasn't been without its challenges. In the fall of 2010, suicides spiked in Andhra Pradesh (whose capital is Hyderabad). The Andhra Pradesh government blamed the suicide increase on microfinance banks, whom they said were offering predatory loans to farmers who could not repay them and were then driven to take their own lives. There's no evidence that SKS caused the suicides, but the news did result in SKS losing its luster. Through the crisis, SKS lost 90 percent of its market value on the Bombay Stock Exchange, and the SKS brand became so fraught that the company changed its name.

Other complications occurred when Unilever acquired Ben & Jerry's in 2001. At first the move was lauded as a victory for capitalism, since the ice cream company had set a new standard for how socially responsible companies should be run. For example, the brownies in their Chocolate Fudge Brownie and Half-Baked ice creams were made by formerly incarcerated bakers at the Greyston Bakery in New York, and the macadamia nuts in their Rainforest Crunch were fair-trade sourced.

Yet over time, Ben & Jerry's supporters started accusing the company of "greenwashing"—suggesting that the company was promoting social impact as a marketing tool, without embracing it as a core practice of the company. As the company grew, it could not source all its brownies from Greyston, only some of them. Unilever discontinued Rainforest Crunch because it was too expensive to make. Scale has tradeoffs: today, Unilever—in large part due to Ben & Jerry's—is by far the largest fair-trade product sourcer in the world,[70] increasing the income of farmers across the world by millions, but not all their products are fair trade.

In both the cases of Ben & Jerry's and SKS, as the firm grew, the company often faced difficult decisions between company growth and social impact. But bigger may not always be better: I asked Vikram Gandhi, an investment banker who handled the SKS IPO, what went wrong, and he said, "The company wasn't growing like a bank. It raised all this Silicon Valley money and was trying to grow as fast as a tech company. In its desire to look like a Silicon Valley tech company, it lost an understanding of the problem it was trying to solve."

WE KNOW WHAT THINGS COST; WE NEED TO VALUE WHAT THEY ARE WORTH

Growing a successful one-pocket business is hard and complicated, and it only grows more complicated as the business becomes more successful. Yet one-pocket thinking will be necessary if we're going to solve the problems we have. We can't create problems with 95 percent of our resources and expect 5 percent of our resources to solve them. Just as we spend billions of dollars finding the next great pro athlete but almost nothing finding the next great entrepreneur, we spend billions of dollars trying to develop mortgage-backed securities or a new financial innovation but almost nothing valuing what things are worth.

We will be more successful, and happier, if we are able to appropriately value social and environmental risk. If a company pollutes, we shouldn't make a moral case; we should make an economic case. We ought to be able to value the company's reputational hit in advance of the next Deepwater Horizon, since an estimated 80 percent of any company's market value is their reputation. But we're not investing in ways to price social and environmental risk today.

The question of what things are worth is harder than the question of what things cost, but we claim we want to address them "someday." The next section will focus on practical ways to take that next step. In the words of Tony Carr, a mentor of mine, "Someday is today!"[71]

PART III

SOMEDAY IS TODAY

How to Overcome Innovation Blind Spots

Someday is today!
  —Tony Carr

The second-best time to plant a tree is now.
  —Chinese proverb

I know one thing: that I know nothing.
  —Socrates

The first part of this book highlighted the blind spots that are hurting our innovation economy. The second part described ideas and illuminators that are helping us see into blind spots. This third part of the book is focused on you, and, if you buy this argument, what you can do next. The answer is different depending on who you are: whether you're an investor, work in a big company, or are a startup founder. This section has specific chapters for each.

We've seen that blind spots are bad for investors, bad for companies, bad for entrepreneurs, and bad for society. But we all have blind spots (I know I certainly do!), and because we're human, we'll never be able to eliminate them all. This section focuses on how we succeed in spite of our blind spots: by being aware of where we are blind. In other words, we need to embrace the wisdom of the Greek philosopher Socrates: "Know that which you do not know."

In innovation, it's better to be specific and wrong than vague and right. This final section is meant to be tactically helpful. Whole chapters might not apply to you. You might not like specific ideas. Some parts might be far too tactical, or too in the weeds, for you to care. This section will also demonstrate specific strategies that have been helpful as I've tried to overcome many of my own blind spots.

To frame this section, I want to tell you the story of an entrepreneur who went from being a social worker to building a billion-dollar company, largely by being aware of her own blind spots, and in the process, created a secure retirement and wealth for employees, investors, and executives alike.

Kim Jordan is the founding CEO of New Belgium Brewing. She attended Colorado State University, in Fort Collins, Colorado, and then launched a career as a social worker in the '80s.[72] She started working primarily with single mothers who were trying to get their lives on track. Kim remembers, "I learned that the most important way to be happy is to codify who you want to be: What do you care about? And how can all aspects of your life—work, family, home—reflect that?" Kim recognized early on that the secret to happiness was one-pocket thinking.

Kim began dating Jeff Lebesch, and both were fans of beer—Jeff was a home brewer. In 1988, they took a trip to Belgium, where they toured breweries on bikes, and decided to start their own brewery back home. The name would be New Belgium. Their first act was to apply the principles Kim learned in social work: "We took a hike to a beautiful place and talked about what we wanted to be as a company. Then we codified the values and behaviors we wanted to have."

New Belgium's core values remain unchanged from their founding, and include "environmental stewardship: honoring nature at every turn of the business" and "balancing the myriad needs of the company, our coworkers, and their families." (Twenty years later, as CEO, Kim still referred to every person at the company as "my coworker.")

When Kim and Jeff started New Belgium, they didn't raise outside investment. They took out a second mortgage on their home and applied for every new credit card they could. One day, a coworker, Brian Callahan, announced that he wanted to leave and start his own brewery. Kim and Jeff knew they couldn't afford to lose him, so they made a handshake deal with Brian for

10 percent of the company if he agreed to stay. Over time, Kim and Jeff started distributing more shares to coworkers. In 2008, Kim and Jeff divorced, and Jeff wanted to figure out how to sell his ownership without impairing the mission of the company. They thought, "Why not sell to our coworkers?" The company bought Jeff's shares, then set up an employee stock ownership plan so that any coworker at New Belgium could earn a stake in the company.

Kim noticed that the coworkers who owned the company contributed more value, and she set a goal for New Belgium to become 100 percent employee owned. In 2012, Kim and the other owners in New Belgium realized that dream. As New Belgium continues to grow, every manager and janitor, every brewer and receptionist at the company will have security for their families and a healthy retirement. In a world where the average CEO makes over seventy times the median employee salary, this kind of financial security for all employees is rare.

"A crazy benefit of being an entrepreneur," Kim says, "is you don't know what you don't know. I built New Belgium the way I did because it seemed like the right thing to do—and I didn't know, because I was a social worker, that other people didn't do them that way. When we started to get the virtuous cycle feedback loop—we gave up ownership to our coworkers and we were more successful—we got freed up to do even more of this. It may be that other people think what we have done is weird, or hippie, but in reality it's the right way to run a business."

Kim's story is a perfect example of how you can illuminate innovation blind spots, no matter where you live or work. Kim cofounded New Belgium because she chose an idea and an industry no one else was paying attention to. In chapter 8, I'm going to talk about how you, too, can find better ideas if you learn to think outside the box. Whether you're an investor, a philanthropist, a judge on a business plan competition, or a manager of a bunch of team members with competing ideas, you're possibly overlooking ideas that are right in front of you. I'll discuss how you can revisit the venture capital process and make decisions in a more transparent and productive way. I'll also provide a playbook for how you can make better and more productive decisions.

In a world worried about income inequality, Kim gave her employees at every level a better retirement because she designed a one-pocket investment structure, employee ownership, for the firm. In chapter 9, I'll take the conversation even further and discuss how you can be a one-pocket investor. By focusing on long-term results, you'll be able to resolve the paradox outlined at the beginning of the book by merging your desire to do something good for the world with your belief in capitalism.

Many innovators have great ideas but struggle to grow. Kim was able to maintain her company's innovative edge because she managed innovation within a big institution well. While most of the book has been focused on entrepreneurs and startups, big companies have serious constraints that are unique to institutions. Chapter 10 will focus on how to illuminate blind spots in a big corporation.

Chapter 11 focuses on government. Most innovators view government as the problem, not the solution, but in one-pocket industries innovators and government will need to work together.

And while much of this book has been about investment, many of our heroes, my own included, are founders at heart. Chapter 12 will focus on founders and will be particularly useful if you feel as though you're in a blind spot. I'll explain how you can break through the roadblocks and into the system.

In the final chapter, we'll revisit the question "What happened to the American Dream?" with some ideas on where we can go from here.

CHAPTER 8

How Investors Can Find Ideas Where No One Else Is Looking

One of the greatest regrets in life is being what others would want you to be, rather than being yourself.
    —Shannon L. Alder

Do you wish to be great? Then begin by being. Do you desire to construct a high and lofty fabric? Think first about the foundations of humility. The higher your structure is to be, the deeper its foundation.
    —St. Augustine

Entrepreneurs often think investors have it easy. But investing well is incredibly difficult.

If you're an investor, you're trying to make high-stakes decisions under time pressure, and it's hard to forecast which ideas will succeed. Your inbox is full of hundreds of ideas, and most of the entrepreneurs seem great. It's difficult to give each idea a fair shot, and you feel guilty that you can't help everyone.

Investors' blind spots are almost always the result of good people trying to do the right thing and getting overloaded, rather than someone trying to be actively harmful. In this chapter, I'll outline some simple practices that can help investors manage their blind spots.

First, let's discuss why we pick the wrong innovations. How did Theranos raise $800 million? When we make mistakes, they fall into categories that logic experts call "type 1 errors" and "type

2 errors." Making a bad decision is a type 1 error: if I'd had a chance to invest in AOL in 1987 and had said no, that would be type 1.

Often, the bigger problem is the type 2 error, which happens not when you make a bad decision, but when you fail to consider an option entirely. In other words, type 1 errors occur when you pick the wrong idea; type 2 errors happen when you don't ever look at the right idea. If I assumed there were no good startups in the Washington, DC, area in 1987, I wouldn't have even been looking for AOL. That's a type 2 error.

In this chapter, we'll provide a playbook for dealing with both types of errors. Let's start with type 1—why we pick the *wrong* innovations.

AVOIDING TYPE 1 ERRORS: INVESTING WITH SELF-AWARENESS AND TRANSPARENCY

Type 1 errors happen when we see a good idea but we've unconsciously trained our mind to overlook it. It might come in the form of herd mentality bias ("no one else is in this deal"), availability bias ("this company is too far away"), or in-group bias ("I got a cold e-mail, not a warm introduction"). We rule out good ideas too quickly.

This behavior is very common. Investors don't have time to investigate hundreds of ideas, and it's very difficult to say no gracefully. It's especially hard if you're a good person who just wants to be helpful. But selecting new ideas requires saying yes to some at the exclusion of others. The single biggest complaint I hear from fellow venture capitalists is "I see so many great ideas and can invest only in a few; I wish I had more time to be helpful to the ones that I can't invest in." But very often what creates this frustration is a lack of transparency and communication. And these issues are not only bad for founders; they cause investors to lose track of companies that could grow into potential "yes"es a few years down the line.

Type 1 errors often happen because innovators and investors are not speaking the same language—and don't realize it. Laszlo Bock, former head of People Operations at Google, calls this the "color blue" problem. As Bock describes, colors are subjective: "How do I know when I see the color blue, it's the same as when you see it?" Are you thinking of navy, royal, or baby blue? Different understandings of the same terms can create major misunderstandings.[73]

As an example, let's consider an expression that investors often use: "We invest when a company has reached product-market fit." To an investor, product-market fit is an advanced stage. If you've reached product-market fit, your inbound requests exceed your outbound sales. You are so good that you're growing without having to try very hard.

An entrepreneur might understand the term differently. Here's a common scenario: an entrepreneur builds a company to the point where she's selling a product to multiple customers. She tells herself, "We've reached product-market fit—now it's time to talk to venture capitalists." An investor meets with the company and tells her, "Love your initial progress, but you haven't reached product-market fit. You're just too early." The entrepreneur will be discouraged, interpreting the feedback as "no," when in truth it might just mean "not yet." The entrepreneur and investor can't have a productive conversation around what product-market fit looks like, and how the entrepreneur can reach it. The connection is lost.

The first step to avoiding this error is self-awareness—on both sides. For the entrepreneur, self-awareness means understanding how far along your idea is and which investor might be a match. For the investor, self-awareness means having an honest look at how much true risk you are willing to take and being more specific about what you invest in. Any answer is fine, so long as you communicate it clearly with potential investments. Instead of saying, "We like product-market fit," you could say, "Come back when your inbound requests exceed your outbound sales efforts."

Greater transparency yields better investments. As one way to make investment conversations more transparent, Village Capital developed a framework to help entrepreneurs and investors have direct conversations, which hopefully will illuminate many "color blue" discrepancies.

In developing this framework, we looked to other industries and took inspiration from NASA, which experienced a similar problem in evaluating the level of maturity of technologies. NASA ranks the level of maturity of a technology from 1 to 9 to avoid confusion about stage of development: instead of saying "early-stage technology" or "late-stage" technology, they say "level 3" or "level 9" technology. Each number means a very specific stage of development to all engineers.

The framework, which we call VIRAL (Venture Investment-Readiness and Awareness Level), allows entrepreneurs to identify how investment-ready they are and investors to understand the point at which they want to invest. We've found it a helpful common language to kick off entrepreneur-investor conversations.

A transparent framework for decision-making helps new ideas go VIRAL

The VIRAL framework outlines nine levels that companies go through as they grow—what Tom Bird, a partner of ours, always calls "laps in a relay race." We've included this framework on pages 98–99.

Let's look at product-market fit again, this time in terms of the VIRAL framework. Rather than relying on a vague understanding of terms, the VIRAL scale explains exactly what investors' expectations—and entrepreneurs' progress—means. An entrepreneur that has achieved true product-market fit, on this scale, is VIRAL level 7. Our hypothetical CEO who has sold just a few items would be at VIRAL level 3 ("Value proposition confirmed by customers"). Now, imagine an investment conversation. The entrepreneur comes to the investor already aware of what they need to accomplish to be considered for investment in the future. The entrepreneur says, "I understand you invest at level 7, and I'm at level 3. Here are the things that I plan to do in the next eighteen months: bring on a CTO and bring on two more large enterprise customers (we're already in talks with ten in our pipeline). What else would you need to see from me to be compelling a year from now?"

Transparency empowers entrepreneurs and investors to frame the conversation at the outset. It changes the investor's framework from investment-worthiness—"yes" or "no"—to investment-readiness—"How ready am I to make an investment in this idea?" And the innovator gets three valuable pieces of feedback from the investor:

1. Here are your strengths and weaknesses as a founder.
2. Here is your level of investment-readiness, compared to where we invest.
3. Here are the questions that investors who invest at your current level will ask you, and that you should be prepared to answer.

The entrepreneur can then look for people who invest at VIRAL level 3. The typical incubator or accelerator, in my experience, works with VIRAL 3 companies, as do many angel investors and grant programs. Almost no venture capitalists do. An early level-setting conversation will help the innovator find the right

VILLAGE CAPITAL VIRAL PATHWAY

VIRAL is a tool to describe company maturity for venture-backed businesses. While all companies are different, this is designed to allow companies to articulate their current stage to investors, articulate milestones they need to hit to close their current raise (if they are raising a round now), and what they need to do before their next raise.

Level	Name	Team	Problem and Vision	Value Prop	Product
9	Exit in Sight	Team positioned to navigate M&A, IPO	Global leader in stated vision	Cited as the top solution in the industry solving this problem	Product recognized as top in industry
8	Scaling Up	Team is recognized as market leaders in the industry	Systems-level change validated	Multiple renewals with low sales effort. Customers in multiple markets love the product	Strong customer product feedback in multiple markets
7	Hitting Product Market Fit	C suite as good or better than founding CEO and can stay with company through its growth and exit phases	Impact is successfully validated	Majority of first sales in target market are inbound	Product is built for scale and additional offerings in progress
6	Moving Beyond Early Adopters	Team has proven sales and product dev skills and management ability to support a growing team for scale	Sales validates impact tied to solution and grows as solution scales	Sales beyond initial target customers. Customers love it and are referring the product to others	Complete product with strong user experience feedback
5	Proving a Profitable Business Model	Team has clear sales/ ops understanding and strategy	Evidence of impact tied to solution—the company has evidence that by growing the business, company solves the problem	Target customers love the product and want to keep using it	Fully functional prototype with completion of product for wide commercial distribution in sight
4	Validating an Investable Market	Team has clear understanding of how their target market operates and has strong industry contacts in this market	The company can articulate systems-level change—how this solution would transform the industry	Evidence of differentiation through initial target customer feedback that the solution solves their problem significantly better than others in the market	Team has clear understanding of product development costs and how to build the initial product cost-effectively
3	Solidifying the Value Proposition	Team has technical ability to build fully functional product and has a clear understanding of the value chain and cost structures in their industry	The company can articulate why they're the best ones to solve this problem	Evidence that customers will pay the target price. For B2C, 100 customers; for B2B, 5 customers and conversations with multiple stakeholders in each	Team has built a working prototype and a product roadmap
2	Setting the Vision	Team has senior members with lived experience of the problem and/or deep understanding of their target customer's problem	The team can solve the problem and can articulate its vision at scale—what does the world look like if they succeed?	The team has potential customers who provide evidence that solution solves key pain point—product is a painkiller, not vitamin	Team has a basic low-fidelity prototype that solves the problem
1	Establishing the Founding Team	Strong founding team— at least 2 people with differentiated skillsets	Team has identified a specific, important, large problem	Team has identified their hypothesis of their target customer—the specific type of person whose problem they are solving	Team has ability to develop low-fidelity prototype and has freedom to operate—not blocked by other patents

Market	Business Model	Scale	Exit	Type of funding typically closed at this level	
Clear line-of-sight to industry dominance	Minimum 2x revenue growth for multiple years	Strong unit economics for multiple customer segments	Growth with exit	Acquirers	
Brand established. Hard-to-beat partnerships for distribution, marketing, and growth	MOM revenue meets industry standard	Growth of customer base accelerates month on month	Team has turned down acquisition offer	Close Institutional VC for Recurring Revenue + Growth	
Sales cycles meet or exceed industry standard	Business model validated. Validation of strong unit economics	Evidence of strong unit economics across multiple markets	Team has strong relationships with multiple acquirers		
Supply/distribution partners see their success aligned with the company's success	Sales begin to map to projections. Evidence of decreasing CAC with growing customer base buying at target price	Company has cleared regulatory challenges and (if applicable) is implementing a strong IP strategy	Team has identified specific acquirer(s) or other exit environment	Close Institutional VC for 1st Sales, Market Expansion	
Team is having conversations with strategic partners to capture their market faster/cheaper than the competition	Financial model with evidence of valid projections to reach positive unit economics	Vision and initial evidence of positive unit economics in two markets	Inbound interest from large strategics	Close Round with Angel and Early VC	
Evidence of $1B+ total addressable market	Team has financial model with cost and revenue projections articulated and a strategy for hitting these projections	Initial evidence that multiple types of customers find value in the solution or in an extension of the product that the company is well-positioned to develop	Evidence of growth trajectory that could lead to IPO, acquisition, or self-liquidating exit	Friends and Family, BootStrap	Angel/Seed Funding Starts
Initial evidence through sales that team can capture initial target market	Team can articulate projected costs along the value chain and target cost points to reach positive unit economics	Clear strategy to move to multiple markets	Initial evidence that the solution already solves the problem better than any incumbents		Grants for R&D (Hardware)
Team understands any regulatory hurdles to entering the market and has a strategy to overcome them	Company can point to pricing and business models of similar products in the industry as further evidence that their revenue assumptions hold	Initial evidence that multiple markets experience this problem	Vision for growth has company solving a large piece of the global problem in 10 years		
Team can clearly articulate total addressable market, the percentage they will capture, and initial target market	Team has identified an outline of revenue model	Team has identified multiple possible markets or customer segments and has aspiration to scale	Team understands what an exit is and has a vision for how they will ultimately provide a return for their investors		

capital at the right time—and strengthen the investor's network and pipeline down the line.

The one-size-fits-all nature of the venture capital process leads to type 1 errors. Too often, investors will pass on the best ideas because "they're not ready." The first time you see an idea may not be the right time for you to jump on it, but a transparent conversation like the one the VIRAL framework allows will let you maintain a good relationship with a potential opportunity—and add value to all parties along the way.

Avoid type 1 errors by changing the decision-makers

The other way to avoid type 1 errors is to change who you have making decisions. I wrote earlier about the understandable, but often unhelpful, bias that people are more likely to invest in the people and places they know and understand. Whether you're investing, making grants, or allocating resources to new ideas for your company, make sure your decision-makers reflect the results you want.

At Village Capital, one way we democratize the process is through peer review, and we've learned that the structure matters as much as the makeup. From 2010 to 2016, we and our partners have invested in over a hundred companies using the peer review process. We've learned through iteration that to avoid cognitive bias, we had to structure the process in a transparent way. We now use the VIRAL framework to undergird the process. Entrepreneurs evaluate one another using the VIRAL categories, with their rankings made public, and entrepreneurs don't score themselves. So far we're seeing a 90 percent survival rate (compared to 50 percent in the average process), and seven times the revenue growth and additional capital raised compared to a control group.

Other innovators are looking at different ways to get new decision-makers in the process. Many investors target women-run and first-time fund managers who may have a more difficult time fundraising, because the evidence shows they outperform. The Kauffman Fellows program, a network of emerging venture capital leaders; the University Venture Fund, the country's largest student-run venture fund; and Kapor Capital, which intentionally places women and people of color in investing roles, are different examples of strategies that aim to get different decision-makers into the venture capital process.

AVOIDING TYPE 2 ERRORS: "IT'S NOT WHO YOU KNOW, IT'S WHO YOU GET TO KNOW"

Most of the stories we've discussed in this book can be described as type 2 errors. For years, Jerry Nemorin was in a type 2 blind spot, because most investors were not looking for a black entrepreneur solving "poor people problems" in Charlottesville, Virginia. Jim Sorenson was in a type 2 blind spot until he learned that his company could provide a vital service to the hard of hearing.

We've also discussed a couple of ways to get around type 2 errors. When Steve Case first got on a bus to go across the country and find the "Rise of the Rest," he was launching a type 2 solution. When Bob Pattillo created a system to empower small-scale entrepreneurs in emerging markets, that was a type 2 solution.

Type 2 solutions share a common trait: they are proactive. They involve going out and finding ideas—and the people and places from which they come—as well as viewing those ideas through a different and possibly unfamiliar lens. There are no shortcuts to avoiding type 2 errors; you have to invest the time in building the pipeline you want to invest in.

The first way we can avoid type 2 errors is to make sure that the way we screen for good ideas isn't exclusive. When professional sports teams evaluate athletes' potential, they look at a range of physical, psychological, and emotional characteristics. When we evaluate entrepreneurs, we look only at their resumes and what they've done with their business—an assessment framework that may cause us to fall victim to massive cognitive bias. We need to get better information on entrepreneurs than a CV and a pitch deck provides in order to deliver better results.

In the past few years, we've been trying something different at Village Capital. In 2016, my colleague Brittney surveyed Village Capital alumni (over five hundred entrepreneurs) in order to determine whether certain personality traits were more linked with the ability to be a successful innovator. She found that many traits you might expect to predict level of success (introvert or extrovert; organized or messy; nice or jerk) weren't correlated in any direction with firm success, but a few surprising traits were. The trait most strongly correlated with success was self-awareness. Let's say an innovator is disorganized, but she's aware of it. Or an entrepreneur is a jerk, and he knows it. Both are fine—and positively correlated with success. The second trait most correlated with success is whether a firm has a female cofounder. Based on the data, here's my top piece of advice to any guy starting a company: be more self-aware, and get a woman as a cofounder!

We now use this data to replace the resume, which we think has no predictive power for a founder's success. To forecast the potential of founders across the board, Brittney developed a survey we call STAR (Startup Team Aptitude and Readiness) that we implement when we're screening for new ideas. Instead of asking for a "warm introduction" or looking at an entrepreneur's resume, we screen teams for personality traits that seem to tip off success.

Whether it's a resume-blind application process, a psychometric test that applies the same tools to everyone, or another process, as you select and invest in new ideas, think of ways to consider whether they have potential—not just whether they fit the pattern.

PLANTING TREES NOW

During my two years at the University of Oxford on the Marshall Scholarship, I lived at New College. At Oxford, a "college" is a dorm, dining hall, and faculty group all in one, and New College, despite its name, is one of the oldest (founded in 1379, over a hundred years before Columbus's voyage to the New World).

New College is fantastically old—many Hogwarts scenes for *Harry Potter* were filmed there—and if you're having dinner in New College's five-hundred-year-old dining room and look up, you see a ceiling the size of a football field that has massive oak beams that span the width of the roof. Around a hundred years ago, the story goes, the old roof beams started to crack, and the New College administration started looking all over the United Kingdom for trees that might be large enough to replace the roof. They found a forest near Oxford with trees that would be ideal. When they looked up who owned the forest, they found that New College actually owned the plot: college leaders had planted the trees hundreds of years ago, anticipating necessary repairs to the roof generations later.

As the proverb says, "The second-best time to plant a tree is now." If you haven't already planted trees, you can't harvest them. You can avoid type 2 errors by investing in pipeline. Taking a cue from the way that college athletes are recruited, Jim Clifton, the CEO of Gallup, developed a test for entrepreneurial aptitude. Jim and Gallup launched pilots in Lincoln, Nebraska, and in Detroit to test high schoolers, regardless of background, on their ability to build a business. Kids who tested in the top percentiles receive full college scholarships, with no strings attached. With a college education and no student loans to repay, these entrepreneurial kids will have the freedom to start a business.

Another way to avoid type 2 errors is to invest in a pipeline even when you're not going to support the people in it directly.

For example, the Techstars accelerator provides cash and support to underrepresented entrepreneurs who may not be investment-ready. Skeptics will say, "You can't just give innovators cash. You need to build a support system around them, otherwise you're setting them up for failure." Later in this book, we'll discuss why you should invest in ecosystems, not just specific ideas, if you want to avoid blind spots.

But there may be evidence that just planting seeds in a pipeline will yield better results. The World Bank conducted a study in Nigeria in which 720 entrepreneurs were randomly selected to receive $50,000 grants. The firms that received grants were 37 percent more likely to survive, and 23 percent more likely to grow to over ten jobs. Perhaps most importantly, giving cash to entrepreneurs who didn't have access to capital created jobs at an adjusted cost per job of about $28,136 less than other government programs.

This is just one study in one country. I'm currently working with partners to replicate this study in the United States and learn what happens. But fundamentally, smart people with great ideas have the ability to create jobs and economic growth, but they are overlooked because of our system. To change the system, we need to invest in the ideas we're overlooking.

If you want to change the way you find and select ideas, and these initial thoughts are encouraging, I've put together some resources for you. Go to innovation-blindspot.com to learn more.

CHAPTER 9

HOW DO I BECOME A
ONE-POCKET INVESTOR?

Know what you own, and know why you own it.
—Peter Lynch

Organization can never be a substitute for wisdom and judgment.
—Louis Brandeis

An Iowa-rooted army brat who still polished his shoes religiously every night, just as he did during his four years in the Army, Bryce Butler was wondering what his next career move should be. As pastor of a church in Louisville, Kentucky, Bryce regularly thought about creative ways to use the church's resources to help improve its local neighborhood of Shelby Park, which was, in 2011, one of Louisville's poorest neighborhoods. According to the Criterion Institute, churches and other religious institutions are a major player in the global economy—they own 1 percent of the real estate in the United States, employ 1 percent of the population, and are the recipients of 50 percent of charitable donations.[74]

After learning more about the community, Bryce decided to leave his job at the church to pursue a few ideas about how to improve his neighborhood and his city. He joined a local foundation, Blue Sky, and started getting involved with organizations in his neighborhood. One of the foundation's charities, Scarlet Hope, took meals to women working in Louisville's twenty-three strip clubs. The founder, Rachelle Starr, wanted to go a step further and open a bakery to provide living-wage jobs for these women so they wouldn't have to work in adult entertainment. But Scarlet didn't have enough cash to start her business and the banks wouldn't make a loan.

Bryce noticed something curious: the organizations Blue Sky was supporting were more interrelated than he would have thought. He imagined a woman who used to work at a strip club instead working for a living wage at Scarlet's Bakery, which an investor could support, and living in an affordable home in Louisville, which an investor could also back. He had unintentionally created a portfolio in his mind. Bryce saw the future. To invest in this portfolio, he founded a firm he would call Access Ventures, in the process becoming one of the world's foremost one-pocket thinkers that you've likely never heard of.

WHAT DEPLOYING A ONE-POCKET PORTFOLIO LOOKS LIKE

If you have a 401(k), think of the "pie chart" report you get on how your investments are doing. You'll see a certain percentage of your investments in stocks, some in bonds, some in "fixed income," some in "alternatives," some in "real assets" (real estate). The chart shows how all your assets are invested, but it may not tell you what your money is actually doing in the world.

Bryce believes, as I do, that the hollowing out of communities poses an existential risk to American society. He had a vision of building a one-pocket investment strategy, starting in Louisville, which could then be a model for other communities that had been gutted and needed quality jobs. The real estate part of the pie chart would be affordable housing. The fixed income investment would be small business loans in groups like Scarlet's Bakery. The stocks would be in companies that created quality living-wage jobs in the communities. And the "alternative investments" would be in startup entrepreneurs.

To realize this vision, he worked with two investors, Ann DeRosa and Chris Knapp (who also helped Victoria Fram and me launch our investment fund at Village Capital), to design an institutional-quality portfolio whose allocations would match any endowment or pension fund in the world. The most important difference: every dollar of the portfolio, not just 5 percent, was invested with the intention of creating quality jobs in Louisville.

Investing consists of risk, return, and diversification. The smart investor looks at the risk and invests where they believe they can get a return that justifies that risk. Right now, blind spots in our markets cause us to ineffectively evaluate financial risk. The best investors over the next generation will be the ones who appropriately evaluate social and environmental risk.

First you need to ask: What problem are you solving?

Bryce wanted to deploy the capital he had raised for Access Ventures in what the investment world knows as "asset classes," or categories of risk and return. By looking at Bryce's portfolio, you can learn what it means to be a one-pocket investor.

Public equity

Public equities are stocks. In Bryce Butler's mind, the tyranny of quarterly earnings in the stock market creates long-term risk for both the companies and the communities in which they're based. Most stock market investors obsess over quarterly earnings: who's making the most money today? But the largest investor in the world, Larry Fink, CEO of BlackRock, says, "Today's culture of

ACCESS VENTURES' ASSET ALLOCATION

Public equity	Private equity	"Real" assets
Publicly traded stocks in companies creating quality middle-class jobs	Startup investments in companies in Louisville, and financial services technologies across the US	Real estate in Louisville
Public debt Municipal bonds for community-building projects in cities	**Private debt** Small-business loans in communities	**Grants** Ecosystem-building initiatives in Louisville

quarterly earnings hysteria is totally contrary to the long-term approach we need."

Bryce, too, believes that the short-term approach that most public companies take to their communities creates potentially catastrophic long-term risks. In order to drive higher quarterly returns, CEOs feel pressure to automate or offshore good jobs, often decimating the communities they're in. While we don't necessarily see the short-term impact on the stakeholders that the company interacts with, if the 2016 presidential election is any guide, the communities feel angry and dispossessed in the long term.

Bryce wants Access Ventures' capital to invest in companies that invest in their communities. He looks at governance, wages, and benefits to determine who is creating good middle-class jobs in the communities he's focusing on. He ultimately believes that Access will make more money in the long term by investing in the best companies.

Most investors don't price social and environmental risk in public equities until it's too late. One investor we've worked with comes from a family that inherited a great deal of tobacco money.

For moral reasons, she sold her share of the family's tobacco stock in the mid-1990s. After the multi-billion-dollar lawsuits rightly hit the tobacco industry in the early 2000s, her wealth was significantly higher than that of her other family members. She did it because it was the right thing to do, and her family members likely wish they'd followed suit.

But I'm starting to see a change. If you want to invest your public equities along with your values, you don't need to set up your own investment firm as Bryce did. You can consult resources such as BlackRock's ESG (environmental, social, and governance) Factors or screened stocks, or you can pursue specific one-pocket objectives through sites I've outlined on this book's companion website, at innovation-blindspot.com.

I'm seeing foundations think with one pocket most immediately within public equities. In 2015 the Rockefeller Brothers Fund—established originally with stock from John D. Rockefeller's success as the first major oil entrepreneur—made waves when they announced that the fund, which has a mission for sustainability, would divest from the fossil fuels that originally created the endowment.

Private equity

Private equity is direct equity investment in privately held companies. Nearly every venture capital investment into a startup is a private equity investment. The best private equity investors have a very specific focus on the problem they're solving. For Access Ventures, it's startups in the communities where they live.

Access also has a sector focus: startups that improve the financial health of working-class Americans. They've invested in Austin-based Student Loan Genius, helping everyday Americans repay student loans; Houston-based Fig Loans, providing a data-driven alternative to payday loans; and Minneapolis-based Upsie, giving consumers the necessary information to avoid getting ripped off on expensive products like warranties.

In the United States, one-pocket investing is largely restricted to "accredited investors," who have net worths of over $1 million and have very few restrictions for investing in individual companies. (That means that if you're like me and 98 percent of Americans, and are worth less than $1 million, it is very, very difficult for you to personally invest equity in any of the startups we have described in this book.) Although a 2012 law, the Jumpstart Our Business Startups (JOBS) Act, which helped everyday individuals invest in small businesses and startups, made this easier, doing so is still difficult. Yet regardless of your background, you're likely an unintentional two-pocket private equity investor.

Apps can power the entire day of a wealthy, well-educated person in a place like Silicon Valley. Uber takes you to and from the office. Blue Apron delivers pre-packaged ingredients so you can cook your dinner without having to visit the grocery store. And you can get nearly anything you want on demand—including a massage via Zeel—through your mobile phone. But many of these apps are dependent on venture capital subsidies. Uber lost $1.2 billion in the first half of 2016—and passengers paid only 41 percent of the cost, with the rest subsidized by venture capital.[75] Blue Apron has raised $200 million, and Zeel has raised $13 million.

And the pensions of most Americans are subsidizing these perks. Venture capital funds are often raising capital from teachers and firefighters in New Mexico and Minnesota to subsidize food and massages for tech employees in San Francisco. In my experience, the kinds of technology that venture capital is investing in today is doing a tremendous amount for well-educated people on the coasts while doing little for middle-class America. Teacher pension funds—with upward of 70 percent female members—are being deployed into a predominantly white male investment ecosystem, which invests in women less than 10 percent of the time.

These venture funds might say that they are delivering above-market returns, but, as a reminder, that statement might not be true: there's a net 0 percent return across venture capital funds.[76]

You likely have capital invested in these funds. Why are you settling for typically average returns in businesses that create convenience rather than solve problems?

If you—or an institution you're associated with—are investing in venture funds with a two-pocket philosophy, you're part of the problem, however unintentionally. Start asking questions.

If you're a limited partner in a venture fund, ask where they're investing—and why.

If you're on the board of a foundation, ask how 100 percent of the assets of the foundation are contributing to the foundation's mission—not just the requisite 5 percent.

If you're an alum of a university with a large endowment, ask your university whether its investments align with the mission of the university.

If you've got a pension, ask your pension manager where it's invested.

If you have your money invested in a 401(k) or with a bank, ask your money manager for transparency on the stocks, bonds, venture capital funds, and real estate that your money is invested in.

Private debt

Debt is a lower-risk, lower-return investment than equity, but it is a core part of any portfolio. Access Ventures was interested specifically in investing in debt for individual businesses such as Scarlet's Bakery, as well as infrastructure banks that could boost small-business lending across the country. Access created a Growth Loan Fund for businesses like Scarlet's, where banks weren't lending.

For most entrepreneurs, unfortunately, banks are not as active as they used to be. Community bank lending is down 50 percent in the United States, and in emerging markets it's worse: the African lending market is undercapitalized by 84 percent, and India doesn't even allow foreign money to invest in debt, leading to an anemic environment for small-business loans.

But a growing range of one-pocket organizations are providing debt financing. Access Ventures made an early investment in Community Investment Management, a "debt fund-of-funds" that provides debt capital to community banks that are short on funds, and in TriLinc Global, which invests in microfinance in emerging markets.

If you're interested in providing private debt to businesses, it's much easier than private equity. Kiva is a platform that Access Ventures supported in Louisville; if you live in one of a few "Kiva cities," you can invest directly in those you know. Two of the highest-impact unicorns in the last decade, Prosper and Lending Club, are "peer to peer" lending services, where you can lend directly to people you know (or people you don't). The Calvert Foundation helps you invest on a larger scale in cities (such as Baltimore or Chicago) or issue areas (such as refugee-owned businesses or women-owned businesses) that you care about, while making a return.

Public debt

Public debt means public bonds: a theoretically low-risk, low-return financial instrument in which investors buy a bond up front and the government repays them over time. When, for example, the city of Atlanta announces that it is issuing a $300 million bond for a new stadium, what's really happening is that private investors are paying $300 million up front to construct the stadium, and the government promises to repay that $300 million over a fixed period of time (through sales tariffs, hotel taxes, or other means).

Almost all portfolios have public debt, whether it's US Treasury bills, municipal bonds, or other instruments. Access

Ventures is particularly interested in bonds that help rebuild the fabric of distressed communities. What distinguishes a "good" bond from a "bad" bond for Access Ventures? Privately operated prisons, for example, are bad; schools or environmentally friendly projects are good.

Investing in public debt with an eye toward long-term financial and social risk can be a successful strategy. I spoke with one municipal bond trader who, for years, had been monitoring various aspects of inequality and social unrest: for example, police force complaints, or basic characteristics of population health. He had his firm sell their position in any bonds that had negative indicators. His big win: he sold their holdings in Ferguson, Missouri, months before the riots—and the city eventually defaulted on the bond. In a one-pocket world, the cities, states, and countries that are managed with the lowest social and environmental risk are the ones that are the most prosperous.

In the last few years, I've seen an emerging innovation in public debt: social impact bonds, or "pay for success." This new instrument enables private investors to back social service innovations in a way that can deliver better results at a lower cost to the taxpayer. As one example, recidivism from prison costs society dearly. Ex-prisoners who commit another crime and return to prison not only tear apart the fabric of their families but cost the law enforcement and criminal justice systems money as well. Early innovators in "social impact bonds" have created a financial instrument whereby private investors, not grant makers, fund innovative nonprofits that show evidence of helping prevent recidivism. In the structure of the bond, these investors get paid for success. Private investors commit up-front cash to a nonprofit; if, over time, the nonprofit has demonstrated that it can reduce the prison reentry of the nonprofit's clients, the government will pay them a profitable return on investment. In the bigger picture, fewer people reenter prison, and society saves a great deal of money.[77]

If you're interested in social impact bonds, you can look into groups such as Social Finance, The Sorenson Center at the University of Utah, or Pay for Success at Harvard to learn more.

Real assets

Access Ventures owns an entire blended portfolio in Shelby Park, Kentucky, from single-family and multifamily homes to commercial real estate, which they maintain well and rent out at a fair market rate. They have developed and filled in vacant lots, and view these real estate holdings as reinforcing their other investments. People who work at Scarlet's Bakery live in Access's real estate holdings. Startups that launch in Shelby Park work out of the Park, a shared office space that Access owns. Bryce knows that if the ecosystem succeeds, their real estate holdings will, too. As we'll see in chapter 13, entrepreneur Dan Gilbert has a similar approach to real estate in Detroit.

Real assets, or physical holdings, are part of any portfolio. They might be real estate or other commodities. Some investment firms that care a great deal about environmental sustainability buy large forests, manage them well, and then sell small, well-managed parts of real estate within the forest; or they buy farmland to produce food sustainably over the long term.

Grants

Access Ventures, in partnership with local foundation Blue Sky, promotes grants, too, as a one-pocket strategy, with a specific eye toward ecosystem building: they want to bring their 5 percent grant budget and the mission of their 95 percent investment allocation into alignment.

For example, Blue Sky made a grant to bring Kiva, an online platform that enables small-business lending, to Louisville for loans too risky for Access. They also brought Endeavor, a nonprofit that helps "scaling-up" entrepreneurs in less-developed ecosystems, to Louisville. And support from Access has allowed Village Capital's agriculture practice to be headquartered in Louisville—a far more strategic place for agriculture entrepreneurs than Silicon Valley.

I've seen other foundations use grant funding to provide support directly to companies in the early days—typically VIRAL levels 1 through 3, using the framework we discussed in chapter 8. Organizations such as the Lemelson Foundation, VentureWell, the DOEN Foundation, and the Shell Foundation support inventors who have hardware and technology to develop.

Grants are especially important if you're developing a company that is capital intensive. New manufacturing companies, for example, typically need grants in order to make their physical product. Clean energy technologies or medical devices have a much more difficult time raising capital than software companies because they may need longer time horizons to take their idea to market.

CHANGING THE PHILANTHROPIC STATUS QUO TO ONE-POCKET INVESTING

Access Ventures is a model others can replicate. As mentioned in chapter 7, every September, several thousand people gather in San Francisco for SOCAP—a conference that bills itself as the "intersection of money and meaning." Every major corporation and investment bank has a presence, and you'll likely find many of the people in this book there, too. Rosa Lee Harden, the cofounder of SOCAP, once quipped, "We should just rename this conference 'Everybody here: just do what Bryce is doing.'"

While most foundations are two-pocket thinkers, a few innovators are leading the way in the one-pocket world. For over forty years, some foundations (notably the Ford and MacArthur

Foundations) have been taking advantage of the opportunity to invest in enterprises that are aligned with their mission. A program-related investment (PRI) is permitted under IRS rules and enables foundations, instead of making a grant, to invest in a for-profit business, provided that (a) the company aligns with the charitable purpose of the foundation (e.g., if your foundation is set up to promote economic growth in Wisconsin, a startup in Milwaukee could be eligible), (b) the investment is not used for lobbying, and (c) the primary goals for the investment are not to generate a profit (though a foundation is permitted to generate a profit).

In 2015 the Ford, MacArthur, Kresge, and Kellogg Foundations all announced intent to invest their endowments in alignment with the foundations' missions. In 2017, the Ford Foundation announced that $1 billion of its $12 billion endowment would be invested in mission-aligned work, one of the largest one-pocket moves a large foundation has ever made. And the $300 million F.B. Heron Foundation announced that 100 percent of its endowment was now aligned with its mission. Still, fewer than 1 percent of US foundations have ever made a PRI.[78] Most foundations fear that a PRI might jeopardize their charitable status, though the IRS released clarifications in 2010, 2012, and 2015 that stress that PRIs in for-profit businesses that are aligned with the objectives of the foundation are an acceptable philanthropic tool.

As for who is impact investing: you've probably heard of the Giving Pledge. Bob Pattillo and others are part of a similar club called the 100% Impact Network: a group of individuals who have dedicated all their assets, not just their foundation's worth, to one-pocket impact. And a new wave of people are structuring all their resources in one-pocket ways. When other successful entrepreneurs would have set up a charitable foundation, eBay founder Pierre Omidyar established the Omidyar Network, a one-pocket, for-profit LLC; in 2015, Facebook founder Mark Zuckerberg and Priscilla Chan followed suit in establishing the Chan Zuckerberg Initiative. Both entities make grants as well as investments.

INVESTMENT STRUCTURES THAT MAY WORK BETTER FOR ONE-POCKET INVESTMENTS

One limit to one-pocket investing may be the structures we use. Fin Gourmet in Paducah, Kentucky, ran into this very dilemma. We wanted to invest in Lula's fish processing company. We couldn't invest in debt, as the risk of the company going bankrupt seemed too high. We also didn't want to invest equity: Fin Gourmet was an inherently local business, and we did not see it reaching the scale that would have an "exit."

We decided to go with another strategy: royalty-based financing. This is a very common investment structure used in books, movies, and restaurants. The investor provides cash up front and then receives a share of the revenue. In Lula's case, we invested $50,000, with a goal of receiving 5 percent of the company's top line revenue until we tripled our money. This style of financing is less risky than equity and has a higher upside than debt—and Fin Gourmet gets to retain ownership of the entire company.

Venture firms across the United States—such as Lighter Capital, Revenue Capital Management, Fledge, and New Hampshire Community Loan Fund—frequently invest through royalty-based financing. And GroFin, a small-business investor in the Middle East and Africa, has invested nearly a billion dollars using a revenue-sharing arrangement.

If you're an entrepreneur, offering an investor a share of your revenue may be a way to get the cash you need now—and incentivize investors to help you increase your revenue rather than just flip your company.

Building a One-Pocket Company Makes the Team, the Business, and Society More Successful

New Belgium Brewing Company, which we discussed at the beginning of this section, is now the third-largest brewery in America and a leader in the craft beer revolution. New Belgium is also a billion-dollar unicorn—but unlike Instagram or WhatsApp, New Belgium structured itself so that coworkers share in the wealth creation and distribution.

New Belgium's employee stock ownership plan (ESOP) is a type of innovation that addresses the income inequality and shrinking middle class that plagues society. We live in a world with growing corporate consolidation and a dramatically expanding gap between rich and poor. New Belgium's employee ownership plan is one example of how greater wealth can accrue to more people. What if you could earn shares in Uber for every ride you gave, or in Airbnb for every guest you hosted?

We don't see more ESOPs because our current investment world is "one size fits all." One investment banker I spoke to at a well-known bank investigated how ESOPs could create more middle-class wealth. He discovered that ESOPs, if structured thoughtfully, are relatively a straightforward model for founders who want to sell shares in their company to members of their team. He asked his bank, "Why don't we do this more often?" He learned that the fee incentives that investment bankers received from ESOPs were substantially lower than they would be for a straight transaction: as a result, investment bankers had no incentive to do the hard work of helping founders sell their companies to their team members.

If you're a founder who's building a company you want to last, you're probably in the best position to fix this problem. Look at ways in which you can make your coworkers literally invested in your success through employee ownership. And if you're invested, look at an ESOP as one potential way to create value. No matter how much money you have, if you start asking questions about where the money you control is invested, you're in a position to change the status quo.

The best news: opportunities to be a one-pocket investor are growing. If you're reading this, and want to become a one-pocket investor, go to innovation-blindspot.com, where I've put more resources to help you combine what you do and why you do it.

CHAPTER 10

HOW DO I ILLUMINATE BLIND SPOTS IN A BIG COMPANY?

This "telephone" has too many shortcomings to be seriously considered as a means of communication. The device is inherently of no value to us.
    —Western Union internal memo, 1876

I think there is a world market for maybe five computers.
    —Thomas Watson, chairman of IBM, 1943

The horse is here to stay but the automobile is only a novelty—a fad.
    —President of the Michigan Savings Bank advising
      Henry Ford's lawyer not to invest in the Ford Motor
      Co., 1903

Most of this book so far has centered on relatively small institutions: entrepreneurs and the venture capital investors who back them. I've been focusing on startups because they are at the leading edge of innovation.

But I also recognize that, among most entrepreneurs, there's somewhat of a blind spot around the value of big companies. When thinking about big companies, entrepreneurs often feel competitive—"I want to disrupt that company"—or antagonistic—"Those big corporate managers don't know what they're doing; they don't even know how terrible they are at X, Y, and Z!" Ultimately, the conventional wisdom—which I myself am guilty of subscribing to sometimes—boils down to "Entrepreneurs are innovative and inherently good, and big companies are stupid and inherently bad." This is wrong.

Big companies will always be part of the economy. Seventy-five percent of people in the United States work for a big company, whether it's Accenture, IBM, Microsoft, Ford, or Johnson & Johnson. Even if you have an entrepreneurial mind-set, you might want to work for a big company to get top-flight management training, pay off your student debt, support your family with a predictable income, or follow your spouse or partner to another city. A lot of people just like working for big companies. (Or maybe they hate them but can't afford to drop that steady paycheck and join a startup.)

What causes big companies to fail are blind spots. One of AOL's biggest competitors at the dawn of the Internet was GE—whose product, GEnie, got beat by the young startup, despite having greater resources. Fifty years ago, Kodak was one of the most valuable companies in the world—until it was disrupted by the digital camera, which in turn was disrupted by the smartphone. The most depressing part: Kodak had an innovator on staff named Steven Sasson who had designs and ideas for the digital camera well before it hit the marketplace. Kodak told him, "No one would want to look at pictures on a television screen." In 2012, Kodak filed for bankruptcy.

If you're working in a big institution, it's likely that many of the blind spots we've discussed in this book are magnified. But you can take proactive steps to illuminate them. In this chapter, we'll discuss how.

BE AWARE OF BLIND SPOTS IN HIRING

The path to better innovation starts with hiring. Yet many organizations, when hiring, fall victim to the same biases that inform investments. And it's showing.

Most early-stage companies have a significant diversity problem: only 8 percent of Silicon Valley employees are Latino, 7 percent are black, and 29 percent are women.[79] Part of the reason for this disparity is likely that our most prominent firms, our most prestigious fellowships, and our top law and business schools rarely consider applicants from outside the elite universities. According to the *San Francisco Chronicle*, Google's recruiters are infamous for dismissing "Ivy-free" job applications.[80]

We know that diverse teams have a competitive advantage: teams in the top quartile of gender diversity outperform teams in the bottom quartile by 15 percent, and teams in the top quartile of racial diversity outperform teams in the bottom by 35 percent.[81] And it's not just gender and race; in chapter 4, we talked about how Jim Sorenson turned his company from a failure to a success because he had a deaf team member who saw an opportunity that no one else did. But we're using the same processes for hiring that we have used for centuries. In a survey of over three hundred companies we work with, I found that 93 percent of firms do the same thing when hiring: gather CVs from incoming candidates and interview the most promising ones.

This "one size fits all" process doesn't work. It relies on "fast and frugal" shortcuts like rewarding people who know how to write resumes and interview well, rather than those who can do the job. I get why this happens: when you're hiring, and you need someone immediately, you often receive hundreds of resumes. Some are horrifying for an HR manager to look at—multiple pages, different fonts, typos—and others are crisp, concise one-pagers like US business schools teach you to write. But resumes and interviews often fall victim to the same biases and shortcuts that we've outlined in this book. People tend to hire from their tribe: "He's a great guy—I know his dad" often trumps the patently better candidate.

We haven't innovated in how we build our teams. When we at Village Capital surveyed hundreds of our alumni, we found that 73 percent relied exclusively on their social networks to reach and hire prospective candidates.

A growing number of startups are helping institutions get past their hiring blind spots. I've been involved with one promising company called Shortlist, based in Mumbai and operating across India and Kenya. Shortlist manages job searches in a way that bypasses the resume entirely. Each Shortlist job candidate completes a short skills-based assessment, and then Shortlist's technology matches the job seeker with all open jobs within the Shortlist network. A recruiter could screen for candidates' entrepreneurial qualities, for example, or propensity to take risk. Shortlist is trying to put the CV out of business—and uncover candidates living in blind spots. Similarly, Interviewing.io and GapJumpers are "resume-blind" interviewing companies for technology firms; they don't look at candidates' CVs, but rather at their ability to perform the basic technical skills for the job.

Other startups are trying to bring new people into the conversation as well, such as LaborX ("LinkedIn for the LinkedOut"), which assesses candidates at community colleges, and Pairin (a startup we have invested in), which identifies a candidate's job talents and matches them with an open job, with an eye toward candidates coming from community colleges and looking for working-class jobs.

One blind spot I often see in startups is that because of the low pay, the teams do not have substantial socioeconomic diversity—too many job seekers simply can't afford to work for such low pay while paying off their college loans. I mentioned our investment in a company called Student Loan Genius, which helps employers pay down their employees' student loans as a workforce benefit. Such an arrangement may make joining your startup attractive to prospective team members from different socioeconomic backgrounds.

In her book *Giving Notice: Why the Best and Brightest Leave the Workplace and How You Can Help Them Stay*, Freada Kapor Klein describes how even subtle biases can cause people to feel like outsiders. Studies show, for example, that women are less comfortable having a title like "ninja," and that office decorations consisting of *Star Trek* movie posters and video games can cause women to self-select out of technology jobs.[82] Office happy hours can be a great way for team members to get to know one another, but think more broadly of other ways to engage team members who don't drink or who need to get home to their families. For example, I sometimes take "walking meetings" with team members through the free art galleries in Washington, DC, where our team is based, or we might play games during a lunch break or go exercise after work together.

As important as this is for big institutions, younger companies can also benefit from innovations around what Kapor Klein calls "people ops." When we surveyed five hundred CEOs who had graduated from Village Capital programs, we found that 90 percent did not budget time or money for their recruiting efforts. The best way to become aware of hiring blind spots in any company, large or small, is to invest in developing a team that represents a wide range of perspectives.[83]

ENCOURAGE DIFFERENT PERSPECTIVES

Startups often praise unpaid internships as a bonus, but this workforce practice can hurt your team. As a startup CEO, I used to think unpaid internships were great—"We get free labor from people who want experience!" But over time, I realized that unpaid internships cut out people who need to make money to support their families or cover personal expenses. As Darren Walker, CEO of the Ford Foundation, wrote in the *New York Times*, "We often hear that success is 'all about the people you know'—as if it's just a matter of equal-opportunity relationship building. We rarely talk about how one knows them, or about the privilege that has become a prerequisite to knowing the right people. America's current internship system, in which contacts and socioeconomic status matter more than talent, contributes to an economy in which access and opportunity go to the people who already have the most of both."[84]

The opportunity cost of "free labor" is high. Certainly you have to spend your time supervising and challenging interns. But more importantly, you're missing out on the chance to invest in people who might bring different perspectives, ideas, and networks to your company. At Village Capital, we no longer have unpaid internships because of the short-term cost to our team— and long-term cost to society.

GET DIRECT EXPERIENCE WITH THE PROBLEM YOU'RE TRYING TO SOLVE

In 2009, Dan Schulman, an energetic child of activists from New York City, was standing on a street corner, begging for money. In his career, he had been known as a slick marketer and great communicator, most recently as CEO of Richard Branson's Virgin Mobile, but in a beat-up coat on a cold New York afternoon, it took him five hours to scrape together a dollar.

Dan felt lucky: he was there by choice. Most homeless people live this backbreaking, dispiriting reality every day. Dan had just taken over as VP of Enterprise Growth at American Express, and he was trying to figure out how to grow the business. American Express had always served the wealthiest consumer segment, and growth was flatlining. Dan had wondered whether American

Express could expand down-market, but he realized he didn't know what it was like to be poor. So he hit the streets—literally. He left home with no wallet, cell phone, or cash and spent a stint as a homeless person. "No one paid attention to me on the street," he wrote for the *New York Times*.[85]

Dan had grown up in a family where he wasn't living paycheck to paycheck. He realized that he had a huge blind spot around the financial reality of the average American—and he had a hunch that this blind spot was thwarting his company's innovation. Dan's time on the street contributed to his effort to lead American Express, in partnership with Walmart, to develop Bluebird, a product that offers an alternative to a bank account, with virtually no fees. Dan developed a reputation for understanding the democratization of financial services; in 2016, PayPal named Dan its CEO.

Dan has articulated a one-pocket mission for PayPal: to "ensure financial health for all people."[86] For example, the company has launched PayPal Working Capital. Let's say you run a food truck, and that's your entire income. One week, your kid gets sick, and you need to take off work and pay for emergency medical care. You've lost your income for that week, and you don't have extra cash or a credit card. Your only option seems to be a payday loan of $300 at 300 percent interest. But with PayPal Working Capital, the company can see from your transactions (which they've processed) that your food truck is a reliable income stream. They'll lend you the $300 so you can take off the week and pay for your kid's medical care, because they know you'll be able to repay it. By 2017, PayPal Working Capital had lent over $2 billion.

To recognize blind spots in a big company, try getting experience living with the problem you're trying to solve. One place to start is with your organization's volunteering program. Most companies have two-pocket corporate social responsibility programs or volunteerism programs that have very little relationship to the products and services the companies provide. You might consider changing these efforts using a one-pocket mentality. For example, if you're in financial services, employees could volunteer to help people prepare their tax forms; or if you're a healthcare company, they could work at a community health fair.

Vikram Gandhi, one of the most active impact investors world-wide, got his firsthand experience through volunteering. Vikram grew up in India and lived what he called the "American Dream," going on scholarship to university in the United States. Working twenty hours a week at a major investment bank, he saw all the deals getting done on the golf course. "I thought I had better learn this damn game," he said, "or I'll miss out on all the great conversations."

In an early golf game, Vikram met David Rockefeller, the same man who introduced Bob Pattillo to microfinance. Vikram, too, learned about microfinance, and in his free time, he started volunteering with the Grameen Foundation, spreading the Grameen Bank worldwide. That decision had one-pocket impli-cations for Vikram. When SKS Microfinance and Compartamos both went public through an Initial Public Offering, they chose Vikram and his bank to lead the IPO. Today, Vikram is a one-pocket investor. Volunteering outside your comfort zone may lead to a better career.

LOOK FOR INNOVATION BEYOND YOUR NEIGHBORHOOD

Corporate venture capital firms have been around since the 1960s, often with an experimental flavor. The idea is for big corporations to seek out and invest in young upstarts that can play a strategic role in the corporation's future. Returns are mixed-to-negative compared with the market; 75 percent of corporations say that financial returns are not the primary purpose of their corporate venturing effort. This means that the corporate venture firm likely has more room to innovate. And research shows that in recent years the programs have lasted longer on average, a sign that they're becoming more integral to corporate innovation.[87]

Corporate venture firms need to make sure they're not missing out on blind spots, too. If you're Coca-Cola or Pepsi, you likely won't find the best innovations in the food and beverage supply chain in Atlanta or Purchase, New York; it might be in Orlando, St. Louis, or Fresno. And the entrepreneurs in those places likely won't move to an accelerator you run in your hometown, because they don't necessarily see the value of where you are compared to where they are.

So if you're a big corporation on the hunt for the next big innovation, look outside your backyard. Consider the case of Pittsburgh, which was the wealthiest city in America a hundred years ago; in the mid-twentieth century, the city declined as the steel industry did. But twenty years ago, researchers at Carnegie-Mellon University started exploring the auto industry through its robotics department, and today Pittsburgh is regaining its footing by partnering with larger companies.

In the early 2000s, when Larry Page, CEO and cofounder of Google, became interested in self-driving cars, he and his team found that the best expertise wasn't in Silicon Valley, but in Pittsburgh. And in 2014, Uber hired about half of the Carnegie Mellon robotics department to form the core of its self-driving car department—in Pittsburgh. Pittsburgh, which in the last century has gained, lost, and regained a reputation as a center of innovation, appears to be beating Silicon Valley at its own game.[88]

One more piece of advice for corporations looking for the next big thing: Don't try to solve the innovation problem with yet another traditional business plan competition! Entrepreneurs hate them, and the judges who select the winners have very little incentive to pick the most original ideas.

LOOK FOR THE BEST IDEAS INTERNALLY

The son of a sheep farming family in working-class Leicester, England, Nick Hughes was an unusual sight walking through the slums of Dar es Salaam in 2001. He was an employee for telecom giant Vodafone, and he was on a volunteer project in the Tanzanian city, trying to sign up people for bank accounts.

Nick discovered that the people didn't want bank accounts. They had created a novel workaround to the need for currency: They bought pre-paid calling cards from Safaricom, a Vodafone subsidiary, then used the calling cards as a proxy for debit cards. They'd pay the grocer or doctor using "minutes" as a unit of cost. People would mail cards loaded with minutes to their families in rural areas. Nick realized that, while the phone card system was a brilliant temporary measure, there were certain limitations, like an inability to transfer money. This was something that Vodafone could help with. He eventually convinced Vodafone to give him £1 million to trial the idea that would become M-Pesa and start the "mobile money" revolution. Now people could use their phone, and the M-Pesa app, to pay for everyday items. It was like having a bank account inside a phone.

Customers loved the new mobile money system. Once the system was in place, piloting in Tanzania and Kenya, a young hotel front desk staffer in Nairobi could send money weekly to his mom eight hours away in Northern Kenya, or a coffee farmer in Northern Kenya could be paid instantly for his goods.

While the idea for M-Pesa came from a two-pocket philanthropy trip, Nick's idea transformed Vodafone in a one-pocket way. The implementation of M-Pesa transformed East Africa. Today, M-Pesa processes 70 percent of all transactions in Kenya, and an estimated 18 percent of Kenya's GDP runs through the service every day. A successful entrepreneurial concept solved a very specific problem—access to low-cost financial services—that governments and philanthropy had poured millions into, unsuccessfully. And Safaricom now dominates the market in Kenya because of its investment in M-Pesa.

Here's another example of internal innovation—but this one wasn't heeded by the higher-ups. After graduating from Howard University, Jewel Burks got a job in digital marketing and advertising for McMaster-Carr, an auto parts manufacturer. For her job, she had to take a lot of pictures of car parts. Jewel saw a massive inefficiency: when customers wanted a replacement for a car part, they would mail in the part so that the manufacturer could find an in-house replacement to match. This was costing McMaster-Carr—as well as small businesspeople in her supply chain, such as electricians, repairmen, and mechanics—a lot of time and money.

Jewel saw a solution that stemmed from her job: a photography service to identify which part needed replacing. She pitched the idea to McMaster-Carr, but it never saw the light of day. So she got together with a friend she had worked with at Google, Jason Crain, and they started their own company, Partpic. Jewel is one of only five African-American women to raise more than $1 million in the past ten years, including $100,000 in investment from Steve Case in our spring 2015 Rise of the Rest event in Atlanta. And in the fall of 2016, Partpic was acquired by a major global online retailer.

The lesson here is that the best ideas may reside within your own team, but you may need to restructure the process to find them. Peer review may be one way to achieve this—remember that Managers are often not the best forecasters of which ideas will be successful, but rather Makers, who are closer to the ground. At Village Capital, we take this to heart. We do an annual internal peer review of key company strategic priorities. Front-line team members have the same voice as the CEO when we develop our new initiatives, and I learn what really is and isn't working in the process.

But peer selection is only one potential approach. I've seen other companies use employee engagement tools in which their front-line team members can peer review their own ideas in an engaging way. (The corporate "suggestion box" doesn't usually work!) Quicken Loans, for example, has a full-time team called the "Cheese Factory" dedicated to proactively sourcing new ideas from team members at every level.

Investing in finding ideas pays off. But whatever tool you use, make sure that the people who have direct experience with the problem have a say in which solutions get chosen.

USE YOUR BIG-FIRM EXPERIENCE INTENTIONALLY

You may not love your job in a big institution. Nearly every day, I receive an e-mail from someone looking for a job or for advice about their career. Often these e-mails come from people who already have a good-paying job but feel stifled or discouraged. They say, "I'm working at an investment bank, making good money, but I hate my job" or "I've built good skills at my consulting firm but don't care about what I do every day. I'd love to work at a firm like Village Capital that has meaning." Very often, these people are one-pocket thinkers stuck in a two-pocket job.

I typically have two responses. First, do what you can from where you can. Employees in big companies have time and skills that can help solve one-pocket problems. If you work at a hedge fund or an investment firm, you can work on pricing long-term social and environmental risk of investment opportunities so people can be better one-pocket investors. If you work at a bank, you can help small businesses learn how to get financing: they may be your customers one day. The list goes on.

Second, think about the long game. When you gain experience in a big company, you may be able to start your own one day, as Jewel Burks did. Another example is my cofounder, Victoria Fram.

She knew upon graduating college that she wanted to pursue a one-pocket investing career, but at that time, such firms did not exist. She worked on Wall Street for half a decade to learn how to professionally manage money, and we joined forces after she did a stint at the "Mission Investing" arm of the Gates Foundation.

SUCCESSES IN BIG INSTITUTIONS CAN CREATE NEW INNOVATIONS DOWN THE LINE

Finally, if you're in a big company, promoting successful innovations will create ripple effects you don't expect. Vodafone is still seeing compounding dividends from M-Pesa. In 2007, Nick Hughes started working with Jesse Moore, a young leader then in business school. Jesse worked briefly with Nick's M-Pesa team and then joined the global mobile operators' industry association. When I first met Nick and Jesse, they had founded a firm together, Signal Point Partners, to explore how mobile money could help alleviate poverty worldwide.

Solar lanterns in India and East Africa were popular, but poor families often did not have the pocket money to afford them. Nick and Jesse started a pilot, M-KOPA Solar ("kopa" means "to borrow" in Swahili), to explore whether mobile money could help. The M-KOPA solar light had a mobile phone's SIM card in a central control box, which was mobile-connected to M-KOPA Solar's control center. The company could turn the power on and off based on whether families had made small daily payments via M-Pesa. Instead of needing to pay full price for a $150 home energy system, families could now pay just pennies a day for their required minutes of electricity. When they had paid off the cost of the solar unit, it was theirs to own.

In 2011, M-KOPA raised its first round of commercial investment; four years later, it was the fastest-growing startup in Africa. The firm has raised money from investors such as Steve Case and Richard Branson, as well as from mainstream firms like Generation Investment Management. These investments are one-pocket: M-KOPA's investors expect to make attractive financial returns. And because M-KOPA uses M-Pesa, Vodafone makes revenue off every transaction.

Every corporation wonders how they're going to avoid the Kodak problem—and find the next M-Pesa. The answer: find ideas where you aren't looking. M-KOPA did well in part because Nick and Jesse are brilliant, and they built a great team. But they also didn't sit in many blind spots. Nick and Jesse were both globally connected people who went to Oxford and worked for *Fortune* 500 companies that were willing to invest for the long term.

One outside-the-box idea can transform a whole system. How many other M-KOPAs are we overlooking? There are thousands of innovators, including many in your own firm, who aren't in the spotlight. If you're willing to think about understanding the problem better, building a more diverse team, changing how you invest, and thinking with one pocket, you might be able to see the ideas that are right under your nose.

CHAPTER 11

How Government Can Play a Role in Closing Innovation Blind Spots

Vision without execution is hallucination.
—Thomas Edison

All politics is local.
—Tip O'Neill

In 2015, I was at a restaurant in Nairobi when Barack Obama, the first sitting US president ever to visit Kenya, arrived in the country. The restaurant shut down so the waiters, back-of-the-house team, and even the chef could huddle around a tiny TV in the restaurant watching Air Force One land on the tarmac. I was there to announce Village Capital's first fund in partnership with the United States Agency for International Development (USAID) at the Global Entrepreneurship Summit.

What was the government doing partnering with a small venture capital fund? When Victoria Fram and I started the first formal Village Capital fund, we learned the hard way about the one-size-fits-all nature of venture capital. We wanted the fund to stay small, and thought $15 million seemed appropriate. The market was willing to pay the usual "two and twenty," and we found it hard to make fifteen investments worldwide on an operating budget of $300,000 per year.

In early 2014, USAID, a federal agency charged with administering civilian foreign aid, announced the PACE (Partnering to Accelerate Entrepreneurship) initiative. Unlike past USAID projects, which provided cash directly to nonprofits or businesses, PACE would provide support to intermediaries, such as funds and accelerators, which could leverage significantly more private capital to support entrepreneurs. The work of intermediaries in emerging countries is hard. A few years back we released a study at Village Capital about what Deloitte calls the "pioneer gap": the paradox where early-stage innovators can't find money while billions of dollars in "impact investment" can't find ideas.

We ultimately worked with PACE to design an innovative structure: PACE would make a grant directly to our fund so that we could resource the team appropriately, and we would keep private market management fees at 2 percent so that private capital would come in. With a $2.6 million up-front commitment, USAID unlocked $15 million that otherwise wouldn't have come from the private sector into early-stage startups addressing global challenges. And we'll be able to give over seventy entrepreneurs their first investment.

The federal government—so often a convenient bogeyman for business leaders—worked with us to get past three blind spots at once.

How can government help close innovation blind spots?

Government's role, it can be argued, is to fill in the gaps where business fails. Government is responsible for ensuring a level playing field, and can be a crucial last line of defense when the sometimes-brutal free market takes its toll. Government can also play a proactive—and often underappreciated—role in driving innovation. But how can government encourage an inclusive environment for the most important ideas? In this chapter we'll look at the three main ways that government can help innovators secure their economic future:

1. *Encouraging economic development*: Government leaders have an ultimate responsibility to make sure that the economy is working for their constituents—on the local, state, and federal levels.
2. *Driving innovation*: In some ways, government is the original venture capitalist. While government is not particularly good at creating jobs out of thin air, good government policy can drive innovation by creating a founder-friendly environment and providing cash infusions to big ideas (particularly around the untapped industries—healthcare, energy, and others—that we've discussed in this book).
3. *Leveling the playing field*: At its most basic, government can promote the conditions that are so crucial to the American Dream, so that everyone with a great idea has the opportunity to give it a go.

For simplicity's sake, this chapter will focus on my home country of the United States, but many of these lessons can be applied globally. I've seen innovative policies and great government leaders in communities, cities, and countries across the world.

ENCOURAGING ECONOMIC DEVELOPMENT

I see a few ways that policy-makers can help drive economic growth in their communities.

Build, don't buy

Government has historically played a major role in economic development; federal, state, and city governments have offices that provide cash and tax incentives to bring in new jobs. But although we know that small businesses and new businesses create the vast majority of new jobs, economic development offices tend to focus on getting big businesses to move to their city or state. Government should build, not buy.

But we continue to funnel our resources into the big. One particularly egregious example: sports stadiums. In nearly every big city, an owner of a pro sports team has held the city hostage, demanding a new stadium or else the team will move. My favorite baseball team, the Atlanta Braves, recently got $350 million for a new stadium—even though their current stadium was only twenty years old!

Over the past twenty years, America has replaced 90 percent of its pro sports stadiums thanks to publicly funded dollars. According to Judith Grant Long, fifty new sports facilities—that each received over $150 million—opened between 2000 and 2010.[89] Nearly every politician justified stadium funding by citing the economic growth benefits to the community. Do stadiums create jobs and grow the economy? The answer from over a dozen studies is a resounding "no." As Stanford professor Roger Noll notes, no facility built recently has even recouped its costs—it would take almost one hundred years for a stadium to repay itself.[90]

If you do need to build a stadium, however, make sure economic growth actually happens. I propose that for every ten dollars that a government commits to a pro sports stadium, the private investors in the stadium project commit one dollar to startup entrepreneurs operating in the vicinity of the stadium. Imagine if, alongside the state and municipal governments committing $400 million to a new stadium, the hedge fund billionaire owners of the sports team committed $40 million (it could even be an investment—not a grant) to startups in the area. We'd see an incredible influx of talent to ensure that the stadium had lasting impact even beyond the short-term construction boom. (Of course, I'd also recommend that the investment be peer-reviewed by the entrepreneurs in the community—that would help decision-makers in the communities avoid the politics of "who gets funding" and, I believe, yield better results as well.) The Cleveland Cavaliers, Detroit Lions, and Los Angeles Dodgers have gotten into the entrepreneurship game, all setting up accelerators or entrepreneurship support programs in their stadiums.

We are seeing some encouraging signs of outliers. St. Louis may be disappointed that the Rams moved from their hometown to Los Angeles—in part, because developers were offered $100 million in tax breaks for a new stadium—but there's good news. St. Louis has seen the largest increase in startups over the past five years of any metro area with more than two hundred thousand people. (For the record, Missouri governor Eric Greitens calls stadiums "welfare for millionaires"—providing hundreds of millions of dollars of subsidies to the ultra-wealthy owners of sports teams.)

St. Louis is one of the cities I've focused on over the past few years, and I've seen government play a role in helping startups. The state has been aggressively investing through its own investment fund, the Missouri Technology Corporation. Our partners at the Kauffman Foundation have been regional leaders. And the Arch Grants program has offered startups $50,000 seed financing just for setting up shop in St. Louis.

Issue job bonds

Stadiums don't create jobs, and neither does the government. Entrepreneurs do. But we can learn from how the government finances stadiums to reduce barriers to entrepreneurs.

One idea I have that cities, states, or even the federal government could implement: a "job bond." Today, the government pays private investors to develop all sorts of things: stadiums, schools, housing complexes. If you're a private investor building a stadium, for example, the government can issue a bond: private investors buy those government bonds up front, providing the cash to build the stadium, and the government repays private investors over time through a specific financing strategy (e.g., hotel taxes).

As we've mentioned before, "one size fits all" structural barriers keep private investors from financing most entrepreneurs. The "two and twenty" barrier means that many small companies and startups won't attract venture capital. The problem: most businesses that create jobs are highly illiquid for a while. These startup businesses are often too risky for a bank to lend to, and usually aren't going to grow fast enough, or big enough, to fit into the venture capitalist's box. Finally, because venture capital funds need to return capital quickly, entrepreneurs are much less likely to attract the investment they need if they don't plan to sell in a couple of years.

The bond structure may be one tool that government can use to help entrepreneurs build businesses and create jobs.

The "job bond" would work like this: a group of private investors—individuals, foundations, institutions—would raise a pool of capital to invest in entrepreneurs that has a specific objective (e.g., create living wage jobs in rural Indiana; provide first-money-in financing to small businesses in Alexandria, Virginia).

At the same time, a government (the city of Alexandria, for example, or the state of Indiana) would issue a "bond," or a "pay for success" contract, where the private investors would only be repaid if these companies actually created jobs, which the government would measure through increased tax revenue from the companies (payroll tax, sales tax, retail tax).

Tactically, let's say there's an Indiana job bond focusing on investing in agricultural businesses that are creating jobs in rural areas. Private investors would put up up front capital, let's say $1 million; the bond could finance ten businesses at $100,000 each.

Let's assume the bond invested $100,000 into a business called Ron's Heritage Farms that planned to create new jobs. Since private investors would only get paid back if Ron's Heritage Farms creates good jobs, the state of Indiana would measure increased payroll tax, sales tax, and more from the farm, and pay investors back out of that tax revenue. If Ron's Heritage Farms made $500,000 for Indiana over five years, Indiana would pay bond holders a subset of that increased economic growth.

If the invested-in companies create good jobs in the area of the contract, investors benefit. If the companies don't, investors won't. Everyone's incentives are aligned. Entrepreneurs get access to a new source of capital, investors are incentivized to create jobs in the specific place, rather than capture value, and the state invests in companies that will actually invest back in job creation.

Accelerate the Rise of the Rest

Government has always played a role in encouraging the private sector to thrive everywhere. From guaranteeing the delivery of mail to remote communities to organizing the Federal Reserve System so that not all monetary policy would be conducted in New York, government has incentivized broad private investment in the economy in an effort to ensure that innovation can be churned out of every corner of the country.

But the twenty wealthiest zip codes have seen a 300 percent increase in business activity over the past thirty years, while the rest of the country has seen a decline in firm creation.[91] Government should be encouraging people to invest in communities everywhere, not just the most convenient.

One idea I like: in 2016, a bipartisan group of senators and representatives introduced the Investing in Opportunity Act (IIOA) to encourage new investment in communities that suffer from a lack of business growth. The law would create "opportunity zones"—designated by the governor of a state—and allow investors to temporarily defer capital gains taxes by investing in businesses located in those zones. The IIOA would also allow investors to pool and share risk in specific "opportunity funds," which would be managed locally. Finally, the IIOA would incentivize investors to "build to last," not "build to flip," by exempting investments held for longer than ten years from taxes on capital gains. As of this writing the legislation was still being debated in Congress; whatever its fate, there are many more good ideas like it.

DRIVING INNOVATION

The government built much of the infrastructure of the Internet and Silicon Valley through grant funding, and the government still has a role to play today in building the future. The Small Business Innovation Research (SBIR) program of the Small Business Administration (SBA), the National Science Foundation (NSF), and the National Institutes for Health (NIH) are three sources of potential seed grant funding. For emerging markets programs, the Global Innovation Fund, a collaboration between the United States and the UK, provides a great example.

Government can do things that no other actors can. The Internet and GPS were developed under Department of Defense research projects. America Online, Ben & Jerry's, Apple, FedEx, Nike, and Intel all received financing from the SBA to develop their companies. Yet our civic leaders, while well intentioned, often do not possess—or know how to leverage—the tools to kindle their own entrepreneurial communities. This section contains a few ideas.

Encourage investment through PRIs

The government needs to help program-related investments (PRIs) to ensure that charitable foundations know they can invest in startups that are aligned with their mission. In chapter 9 we learned that only 1 percent of foundations take advantage of this opportunity. The bipartisan Philanthropic Facilitation Act is one idea that would make PRIs easier, and provide foundations more comfort in investing, by enabling for-profit businesses to apply for certification from the IRS that they have a core mission, similar to how nonprofits apply today, which would give private foundations greater comfort that they can access capital.

Make tax policy that benefits innovators, rather than preserves the status quo

Corporate consolidation is at an all-time high. Hundreds of billions of dollars languish like dead inventory in corporate accounts offshore. At the same time, firm creation and R&D spending from corporations is at a low in our lifetimes. For the United States to remain the most entrepreneurial nation in the world, we need to invest in the next generation. Recent offshore movements of companies such as Pfizer are draining the US Treasury and killing the free cash flow of the American innovation economy.

In the run-up to the 2016 election, some politicians called for a tax amnesty so that corporations could pump their dollars back into the US economy. While I understand why many people oppose that idea—saying that corporations ought to pay their fair share—I wonder if incentivizing corporations to invest in growth could generate more prosperity for all. I propose declaring a "Small Business Repatriation Holiday," wherein companies would be allowed one-time tax amnesty to move capital back into the country, provided that the money that would have gone to taxes would instead be invested in R&D in American startups that fit critical national imperatives. For example, if Google has $100 million in bank accounts in Ireland and is afraid of moving it to the United States because of tax liability, the Small Business

Repatriation Holiday would allow Google to move that $100 million back tax-free, provided that $35 million would be used to establish a startup investment fund that fit key identified criteria.

Play a concierge role

A smart economic development policy recognizes that small businesses and entrepreneurs create the vast majority of our new jobs, but the current regulatory environment benefits the big players to the detriment of the startups. The SBA estimates that small businesses pay 36 percent more in regulatory compliance costs than large businesses.[92] While meaningful efforts have been made to reduce and simplify local, state, and federal compliance requirements, not enough progress has been made toward implementation.

A report by the National Association of Manufacturers estimated that federal regulations cost the US economy more than $2 trillion in 2012.[93] In the government's efforts to account for all possible negative outcomes, regulations have become too excessive for small, emerging firms to bear. These regulations also result in a significant rise in costs for small-business owners, the large majority of whom come from the middle class.

Managing compliance can have other detrimental effects on the entrepreneurial landscape. Broadly speaking, overregulation discourages entrepreneurs from launching ventures in the first place. Some 22 percent of entrepreneurs cite regulation as the single biggest inhibitor to growth, ahead of such common challenges as sales, taxes, and the affordability and availability of insurance—up from just 8 percent five years earlier.[94]

One approach to solving the problem is to encourage the government to play a "concierge" role. Realizing that making regulations easier for startups would take too long and be too expensive to change, former New York City mayor Michael Bloomberg set up a program that assigns companies an agent to walk them through the process of starting a company.

Complete deregulation is not the goal (nor should it be). But less cumbersome regulation, streamlined to ensure greater timeliness and responsiveness on the part of government, coupled with lower aggregate costs, is absolutely essential for launching new ventures and nurturing existing ones.

Open up different ways for people to innovate

When policy-makers change how entrepreneurs can access capital, people are able to come out of the blind spots. Take, for example, crowdfunding: a full 50 percent of successful fundraisers are women CEOs, compared to less than 5 percent in venture capital. Globally, there are an estimated eight hundred crowdfunding platforms, and the number is expected to continue to grow significantly through the decade as crowdfunding regulations become easier to navigate.

Recently, the Securities and Exchange Commission (SEC) adopted rules to implement Title III of the JOBS Act, which allows startups to sell securities through fundraising. This gives firms the ability to crowdfund seed funding to get their project off the ground. Crowdfunding is a start—but it's only one part of the larger picture.

LEVELING THE PLAYING FIELD

Government has a responsibility to invest in the next generation. But we currently invest far more in finding athletes than we do in finding innovators. If we're looking to entrepreneurs to create nearly all the jobs of the next generation, government ought to invest in the best entrepreneurs who aren't currently on the playing field.

Give a second chance

It isn't news that America has a problem with mass incarceration. But that means we also have a problem when citizens return to their communities. Formerly incarcerated people are 50 percent less likely to get called back for an interview and thus often struggle to find a job.

In our own society, we can help people who are struggling to get back on their feet through starting a business. People returning to society from prison often have a difficult time getting jobs; entrepreneurship may be a path forward for them. If a mere 10 percent of people leaving prison each year started their own businesses, 6,500 new businesses would be created in the United States every year.

Defy Ventures is one example of an organization that is helping encourage entrepreneurship in prisons. Founder Catherine Hoke has developed a program that helps people returning to society launch a business. In 2016, Defy graduated 1,100 entrepreneurs upon release, and they went on to create 150 businesses. Graduates have a 3.2 percent recidivism (re-incarceration) rate;[95] the national average is more than 75 percent.[96] Recidivism is bad for society, and it's expensive. The government could partner with groups like Defy to bring more innovators into the conversation—while saving taxpayer dollars in the process.

And we may see many of these entrepreneurs improve our criminal justice system. In 2002, Brian Ferguson was well on his way to graduating with a 4.0 from West Virginia University when he was wrongfully convicted of murder. Brian, even as a well-educated returning citizen who did not have a criminal record, still found the process of reentry overwhelming: setting up a bank account, getting a mobile phone, paying taxes—and saw that most returning citizens get taken advantage of by predatory service providers. Brian created Start Line, which helps returning citizens navigate businesses and social services.

In 2007, Frederick Hutson was incarcerated for dealing marijuana. While in prison, Frederick observed officials striking deals with private telecom companies that massively inflated prices for prisoners to call home. Staying in regular touch with families dramatically decreases the rate of recidivism for prisoners returning home, yet costs were exorbitant. Frederick developed the concept for Pigeon.ly, which uses a Google Voice–like technology to cut the cost of prison calls 80 percent.

Catherine, Brian, and Frederick have all created companies that give hope and opportunity to millions of people in prison across the country.

Revise immigration policy

Most headlines about immigration focus on negative aspects, but immigrants contribute heavily to economic growth as well. Despite accounting for only about 13 percent of the population, immigrants now start more than a quarter of new businesses in the United States.

Countless standout successes—Google, Tesla, Chobani, PayPal, and more—were immigrant-founded. Immigrant founders started 52 percent of all new Silicon Valley companies between 1995 and 2005, and in 2017, an immigrant is more than twice as likely to start a company as a native-born American. And immigrant founders are creating massive numbers of jobs: more than 20 percent of the 2014 *Inc.* 500 CEOs are immigrants, and 75 percent of patents developed in American universities had the participation of immigrants.[97]

Yet US immigration policy is not entrepreneur-friendly. In Philadelphia, I heard a heartbreaking story of an Indian entrepreneur who came to graduate school in the United States and wanted to start his company here, yet due to visa issues, he had to go back to India. His e-commerce startup now employs thousands of people in India—jobs that could have gone to Americans.

Companies know how critical talent is and are willing to invest billions of dollars in finding, recruiting, and attracting the best talent in the world. For over a century, the United States has been the country of choice for the world's best and brightest, who have created a better economy for everyone. The country should continue to recruit the best entrepreneurs to remain competitive.

I propose a "stapled green card" to the diploma of any foreign-born US student who wants to start a business here. If you start a business in the United States, you get a five-year green card to make your dream come true. (Of course, your business would have to meet certain requirements in order to avoid immigration fraud.) If you create at least one hundred jobs and are surviving as a legal business five years later, you receive a permanent green card. Just as companies recruit the best entrepreneurial talent, so should the country.

Alleviate student debt

For people who don't come from a well-off background, student loans represent a significant obligation—and a barrier to entre-preneurship. The class of 2015 graduated with a debt of more than $35,000 per individual,[98] over $15,000 more than the class of 2005. With student debt at an all-time high, entrepreneurship is likely to decline.

Startups like MPOWER Financing, based in Washington, DC, can help. Founders Mike Davis and Manu Smadja met in graduate school. Both high achievers, they had significant potential but a thin credit file, and they struggled to get graduate school financing.

Student lenders typically treat a student's background as a liability: students who come from low-income families and cannot access financing are considered a risk. Your FICO credit score—if you're a college student, largely the result of family circumstances you were born into and can hardly control—might direct your destiny. But Mike and Manu saw students as assets, not liabilities. MPOWER helps lenders assess the potential of a student by gathering data on specific traits (GPA, activities, work history, and so on), which enables access to fairer loans and better interest rates for people with little to no credit history. Perhaps most promising, MPOWER is seeing many of its students use their refinanced debt to start businesses.

To take this concept to a broader level, I propose "Startup Student Loan Deferment." If you're starting a new business and you owe on student loans, government institutions (whether it's a federal lender like Sallie Mae or a state university) would defer student loan repayment for a fixed period of time—say, five years—to give students the time and space to develop a business. I think we'd be surprised to see who gets off the sidelines.

Veterans and entrepreneurship: a troubling decline, and a better way

Military training can often be a head start for a career. Indeed, veterans have historically represented a disproportionately high percentage of entrepreneurs in American society: 45 percent of veterans start their own businesses.[99]

Yet one trend is troubling: over the past decade, the veteran share of entrepreneurship has declined by 50 percent. This may be due to changes in the workforce. Older veterans, who are now retiring, started businesses at a much higher rate. This may be because veterans leaving the military today have much poorer social networks and support systems than veterans of the past. Veterans often face challenges in medical care and mental health that may obstruct mainstream business success, and they live in disproportionately rural areas, which mainstream investors tend to undercapitalize.

Yet veteran entrepreneurs can build great businesses. Fred Smith, the founder of Memphis-based FedEx, was a Marine officer who cites his keen observation of military logistics as the inspiration for FedEx. And entrepreneurs can also improve quality of life for veterans: 1DocWay, founded in Philadelphia, is a telepsychiatry solution that provides mental health support for veterans in rural areas. 1DocWay has been one of our most profitable investments at Village Capital.

The US government should develop a startup equivalent to the GI Bill. Veterans can access up to $66,000 for education—why not make the same amount available to them for business investments?

Prepare for the next generation of entrepreneurs

From *American Idol* to the Final Four, kids who want to be entertainers and athletes see an aspirational path to success. Surely we can do as well to source the best entrepreneurs internally.

I launched my first startup when I was in college. I didn't know in high school that "entrepreneur" was a career path; I was lucky to have Bob Pattillo as my mentor. But most kids don't know somebody who can invest in their first startup. The notion of entrepreneurial education at the K–12 level is not new, but we don't have an infrastructure at the local, state, and national levels that functions similarly to how Model UN, Boys Nation, and Girls Nation work for aspiring politicos. I propose a National Entrepreneurship Contest, where each school can submit an entrepreneurial idea and compete at the local, state, and national levels. (To avoid bias in picking "the best," I suggest that the winners be peer-reviewed by fellow students.)

Ultimately, entrepreneurship matters to policy-makers because the people who have capital, networks, and relationships are the ones who will define the future economy. If the only people who have the chance to start a business are the kids of tech entrepreneurs, lawyers, and bankers in New York and Silicon Valley, we won't see, for example, people wrestling with the very serious issues of how technology can automate jobs. If kids from Ohio's Mahoning Valley or West Baltimore, both hard-hit by the loss of manufacturing jobs, get the chance to start businesses, maybe they'll have greater insights into what the one-pocket opportunities for companies can be.

CHAPTER 12

WHAT DO I DO IF I'VE GOT THE NEXT GREAT IDEA?

*Timing, perseverance, and ten years of trying will
eventually make you look like an overnight success.*
—Biz Stone, cofounder of Twitter

So far this book has focused on how people invest. But what if you're an innovator in the blind spot? Maybe you've got a startup that no one is paying attention to, or you're in a big company and have a big idea. My hope is that in reading about what's wrong about the system, you can learn how to hack into it better.

There are loads of good books out there that can teach you how to start a company. Two I recommend are Brad Feld's *Venture Deals*, which is especially useful if you're looking for tactical advice on how to raise money, and Ben Horowitz's *The Hard Thing about Hard Things*, which helps you learn how to be a startup CEO. This chapter is not about how to build a company, but rather about four things you can do to remove yourself from investors' blind spots.

1. HANG A LANTERN ON THE BLIND SPOT YOU'RE IN

Clarence Bethea grew up in Atlanta, just as I did. We're both entrepreneurs, but we've had very different journeys. I grew up with two parents who cared about me, supported me, and invested in my education and well-being. The only memories Clarence has of his dad are of him coming to the house, high or drunk, to beat his mom, and he had to earn money as quickly as possible to get some financial independence. He remembers, "My first job was selling dope and weed. Today, I know how to manage money because in my first job, if I came up short on cash, I was dead."

Clarence was convinced that college wasn't on the table for him, since he couldn't afford it. But he was a gifted basketball player, and he found out that he had a chance for a scholarship to a small college in Minnesota. While there, he coached youth basketball to earn some extra money on the side. One day at basketball practice, one of the parents said to him, "Clarence, I see something in you. Come work for me." This parent was the CEO of a Minneapolis-based *Fortune* 500 company, and Clarence became his mentee.

Clarence says, "I've always been a warranty guy." Growing up when money was scarce, he had to save for months to buy a new TV or a microwave, and he wanted to make sure his purchase was protected. But he learned from being on the inside of the industry that warranties often ripped consumers off. It might cost $40 to insure a TV, but families sometimes end up paying months' worth of savings to buy a $200 warranty. Retailers can make up to 300 percent margins on warranties by not being price-transparent—Best Buy reportedly made $1.1 billion in 2015 on warranties alone.[100]

The more Clarence learned, the more the problem bothered him. Sales associates at retailers often didn't know what was covered, and the warranty itself was dense and hard to understand. Clarence felt that if warranties were more transparent, consumers who needed the extra cash could save a lot of money. He launched a startup, Upsie, as a Kayak-like interface that helps consumers find fair and transparent warranty prices.

Village Capital invested in Upsie, and we've been impressed by the business. The profit margins are great, and Upsie is providing serious value to consumers. But even as I've seen Clarence raise money, I've seen him struggle. As a black guy, solving poor people's problems, in central Minnesota, he's just like Jerry Nemorin: 0 for 3.

The bias against Clarence soon became obvious. A leading venture capital firm loved Upsie and gave Clarence a term sheet—a basic outline of an investment agreement—for $2.5 million. Then the firm started looking for other venture investors to come into the deal. One of these investors ran a background check on Clarence. Clarence is thirty-six, is married, and has a kid, but a criminal charge that was over fifteen years old popped up. "I was young and stupid," says Clarence. But both venture capitalists ended up citing his record when explaining why they ultimately couldn't invest.

I knew that if I had been charged criminally when I was in high school, on the other side of town from Clarence, my parents could have afforded a good lawyer who would have made sure those charges never hit my record. I called an investor I respect, who happens to be African-American. He said, "Investors buy stories, and Clarence is awful at telling his story. He needs to make his past an asset." He recommended that Clarence come right out and say, "I grew up a poor black guy in Atlanta—I even had a criminal record—but I've worked my way up and now I'm running this company."

The lesson: If you have something that you think puts you in a blind spot, turn it into an asset. When you're telling your story, leading with what you perceive to be your weakness will put you in a stronger position than ever.

2. TRUST, BUT VERIFY

Before Village Capital had a fund, and before I even had any team members, I relied heavily on partners to test the thesis of peer selection. We would organize a group of one-pocket entrepreneurs in a city and run a program together to teach them how to make investments. I'd usually raise a syndicate of investment totaling about $100,000 that we'd pre-commit to the companies in the program. The entrepreneurs would then decide who would get investment.

In one early pilot, an investor offered the entire cash amount up front. Yet despite good intentions, the program ended up being a disaster. Throughout the program, the investor did more talking than listening, and his criticisms to startups did more to tear down than build up. When entrepreneurs gave him feedback on what they didn't like about the program, he responded, "I'm the one putting up the money here—do you want the cash, or what?"

At the end of our program, two outstanding women received peer-selected investment. We had a celebratory dinner and, despite the bumps in the road along the way, the entrepreneurs were happy. I was at JFK waiting for my connecting flight when I saw the investor's number come up on my cell phone. Through a call filled with static, the investor admitted that he didn't actually have the $100,000 to invest in the companies. He wanted to know whether I could make a loan to him. I told him that I didn't have any money, and he asked, "Well, could you go raise it?"

This investor had spent the recent months speaking on panels and masquerading as a leading angel investor. How, I wondered, did he not have the money to fulfill his commitments? It turned out he had never had the money to begin with. He said he had secured a pledge from a friend to back the $100,000, but the pledge had fallen through. Now, he was hoping that we could bail him out—he said his reputation would be ruined if we couldn't help.

I was furious. I had trusted him—as had our founders. The only money I had in the bank was what was left from the $65,000 loan Bob Pattillo had given me to cover Village Capital's early operational expenses. Ultimately, my board and I decided that we needed to do what we could to support the entrepreneurs. I still regret that we didn't have more, but we contributed $5,000 apiece as a zero-interest lifetime loan to the companies. I called everyone I knew, and while we didn't raise the full $100,000, we did raise a meaningful amount.

The episode almost killed Village Capital. And it almost killed the two firms that were peer-selected. My biggest mistake was assuming that because the investor claimed to have money, he would deliver. I've worked with many great investors, but I've also come across more than a few who don't have the cash they claim to represent, or who do months of "due diligence" without delivering.

The lesson: Money is fungible, but your time is not. If you're a founder, you should assume the best of people who claim to be interested in investing in you, but don't let them have power over you. Ask what other deals they have done. Ask who they have invested in, how they invest, and how long decisions typically take. If they are willing to be transparent, that's a good sign that they will give you a fair shot.

3. DON'T STOP ASKING FOR HELP

Ben Franklin once suggested that if you want to make a friend, let someone do you a favor. As he says in his autobiography, "He that has once done you a kindness will be more ready to do you another, than he whom you yourself have obliged."[101]

Very often, entrepreneurs who are unwilling to ask for favors get stuck. If you're an entrepreneur, remember that every successful entrepreneur had someone like Bob Pattillo who took a chance on them. Entrepreneur Brad Feld even has a mantra, "Give first," that describes how great entrepreneurial ecosystems work. People who have been successful want to pay it forward.

Take Yvette Ondachi, a Kenyan pharmaceutical saleswoman living in a farming community. She remembers, "I would sit in the doctors' waiting rooms and look at the people around me and think, you know, only 5 or 10 percent of these people can afford these medications." She wanted to solve this problem but didn't know how.

Meanwhile, a farmer friend mentioned that his kids went to a more expensive school than hers did. When she asked how he could afford it, he responded, "There's big money in farming, if you know what you're doing!" He told Yvette a little bit about how he did things, and she decided that she wanted to try her own hand at farming. She asked around and ultimately found another farmer who owned seven acres and was willing to lease one to her.

After her first year, Yvette was making good money using what she'd learned from her farmer friend. She recognized that there was a big business opportunity to be had in aggregating, wholesaling, and selling produce directly to supermarkets and restaurants—the Kenyan version of "farm to table."

Yvette realized that with proper inputs and great market access, she could increase farmers' incomes by as much as ten times, which would enable farmers to buy everything they needed for their families, including medicine. Today, Yvette's company, Ojay Greene, manages the supply chain for some 1,500 farmers. Yvette has received investment from our fund at Village Capital, as well as international entrepreneurs such as Jean and Steve Case. Yvette built a promising business by asking for help from everyone—from farmers to investors—every step of the way.

The main reason founders don't ask for help is that they're afraid people might say no. I've found that a helpful way to frame a conversation is to borrow a phrase from Tom Bird, one of our early investors: "No is my second favorite answer." Of course we want yes, but no frees up time to pursue other options that we would have otherwise spent hoping something worked.

If you want a tactical tool, my brother Henry once taught me a simple formula to ask for help, called GVAP. In any interaction, you should have a GOAL, a VALUE you're proposing, an AGENDA, and PERMISSION. See innovation-blindspot.com for a GVAP template and a sample e-mail I've written to get you started.

The lesson: Ask for exactly what you need, and give people the opportunity to say no. You'll be surprised how many say yes instead.

4. THINK BIG

Every investor has a job to do—they need to make money for their clients, or for themselves, or they want to solve a problem that they care about. The single biggest mistake I see founders make in fundraising is trying to get investors to care about them—but not showing equal empathy for investors. If you want to raise money, you've got to show investors the value you bring to the table.

If you're like the average founder I see, especially if you're in a blind spot, you're hesitant to talk about your ambitions with investors. You might say, "I need only $100,000" because you don't dare ask for more. But as we saw in chapter 3, it's often easier for a startup to raise $800 million than $100,000. In order to get out of the blind spot, recognize that investors are more likely to back a company with a vision for growth rather than one that's trying to raise the minimum amount they need to keep their lights on.

When I see entrepreneurs trying to raise money, they often say, "I've done so much with very few resources. If I got just a little bit more, here's what I could afford." Instead, come to every conversation from a position of abundance: "If I had unlimited resources, here's what I could do." Investors are looking to invest in something that will be a big success.

PART IV

TOPOPHILIA

America thinks of itself as having a few distinct islands of
tech creativity; I now see it as an archipelago of startups
and reinventions.
—James Fallows

How can we close blind spots? Perhaps our biggest blind spot of all is our tendency to look to individual heroes and innovators, rather than communities and ecosystems, to solve our biggest problems. Change will likely come not from the next Steve Jobs or Mark Zuckerberg, but from the thousands of "regular people" who are reinventing their industries and their communities. None of them are big enough to capture your attention like a Silicon Valley unicorn, but collectively they are helping combat the lack of identity, economic belonging, and meaning that so many Americans suffer from today.

From 2013 to 2016, journalists Jim and Deb Fallows traveled to small towns all across America to spend time with the unknown innovators building their communities from the ground up. They spent time with school board candidates in the Inland Empire of Southern California, residents in a successful refugee integration program in Sioux Falls, South Dakota, and leaders building a new startup hub in Erie, Pennsylvania, in the shadow of rusting factories.

The journey led Jim and Deb to draw two conclusions.[102] First, we're reaching the end of a Second Gilded Age, similar to the days of J. P. Morgan and Cornelius Vanderbilt. Corporations and government entities have consolidated to the point that they are indistinguishable, and most people can't find a job or a career in the maze.

Second, the people leading a national turnaround in this country won't be policy wonks in Washington, CEOs in New York, or tech geniuses in Silicon Valley. It will be the thousands of local leaders, largely unsung, who are doing the hands-on work of engaging with communities—leaders that have a range of education levels and a diversity of economic challenges—rather than a monocrop pipeline of well-educated people from Harvard and Stanford funneling more money into well-funded ideas.

Journalist Bill Bishop describes a phenomenon he calls the "Big Sort," in which the so-called best and brightest gather in alpha cities—San Francisco for technology, Los Angeles for entertainment, New York for finance, and so on—while most other communities are hollowed out.[103] The Big Sort has created many of the blind spots we've talked about in this book—particularly, the "one size fits all" mentality that assumes that all entrepreneurs fit the same cookie-cutter Silicon Valley image.

The Big Sort has also created the "bigger is better" mantra, where the only way people who are investing know how to make money is through financial incentives. "Two and twenty" venture funds, as we discussed earlier, incentivize you to invest in bigger, later-stage ideas. Private equity firms are rewarded for buying and consolidating companies, rather than starting new ones. And more than ever, large companies are aggressively buying back shares with extra cash rather than investing in new ideas and startups. As a result, as we discussed in chapter 1, economic dynamism is at a thirty-year low and corporate consolidation is at an all-time high. The people who didn't win in the "Big Sort" got left out.

But I'm seeing hope in a different story. In 2016 we visited Denver on the Rise of the Rest tour. Governor John Hickenlooper, an entrepreneur himself, joined us for breakfast at the Wynkoop Brewing Company, which he had founded nearly twenty years before. The Kauffman Foundation had recently ranked American cities as "best for entrepreneurship," and four of the top ten were in Colorado. Someone asked Governor Hickenlooper why.

He responded, "I'm going to tell you a word you may not have heard before, but it's my answer: *topophilia*, which means 'love of place.'" He went on to explain that the communities of Denver, Boulder, Fort Collins, and Colorado Springs were places that people had invested in, places that gave their citizens a sense of identity and hope. When people find meaning where they live—both the physical location and the ecosystem—they feel the freedom to create. And it's this freedom that will allow us to begin to close blind spots.

In a globalist world, many of us have lost the idea of topophilia; society and the economy have pushed in directions away from a specific, powerful sense of place. But this powerful idea has built individuals, enriched communities, and created breakthrough innovations for thousands of years. In Renaissance Italy they had a different word for the same idea, *campanilismo*—"love of one's own bell tower." Strong, thriving civic cultures in that place and time were indispensable in fostering the groundbreaking art and science of familiar names like Michelangelo of Florence and Leonardo of Vinci.

The loss of that passionate commitment to a place has had a huge cost. Social scientist Robert Putnam, in his famous 2000 book *Bowling Alone*, highlighted how the disappearance of civic associations, from bowling leagues to religious institutions, had played a major part in creating the decline of social cohesiveness—and social mobility. Putnam's 2015 follow-up book *Our Kids* highlights how because of the decline of community, people have far fewer relationships with people outside of their socioeconomic status, which I'd argue further contributes to the "in-group" bias of how new innovators get opportunities.

From religious institutions to recreational activities to civic organizations, the ties that bind people together are breaking down in places like Appalachia and the hardest-hit parts of our cities. And they are often not even starting up in the booming exurbs and rapidly gentrifying hipster paradises in many large cities.

As Americans have grown less connected to any place at all, it's no surprise that the American Dream in many communities has drifted further and further out of reach.

Rebuilding the American Dream is a daunting task, but we need to start with our communities. Most of the heroes I've described in this book think that they are working alone, and that while their individual efforts are important, they are likely too small to matter. But as Jim and Deb Fallows reflected at the end of their journey, "The people who have been re-weaving the national fabric will be more effective if they realize how many other people are working toward the same end."

It's easier for us to celebrate individuals than systems and movements. This is partly a quirk of human nature, since it's easier to remember a face, and partly a quirk of American culture, where celebrity is revered—in some cases for nothing more than being celebrated. When we want new ideas, we look for them to come from the heroes we can recognize. The venture capital process looks for new ideas in the same way.

But the heroes we revere in American history do in fact represent systems of people working together. Contrary to popular myth, Paul Revere never completed his midnight ride: he was captured by the British, but three other couriers he was working with stepped in to finish the job. Davy Crockett organized a band of militia "volunteers" to defend the Alamo. Harriet Tubman coordinated a group of former slaves and abolitionists across the country to create the Underground Railroad. And Rosa Parks was tired of giving in and had the courage to say, "Enough!"—which mobilized a chain of churches and organizations across the South to help bring down segregation. Each of these leaders had a community to back them up.

I propose that the way to close blind spots is by investing in ecosystems, not just specific ideas. Victor Hwang, vice president at the Kauffman Foundation, defines an ecosystem as the inter-relationship of all the parts in an entire system. If you look at Bryce Butler's investment strategy in Louisville, you see that the debt that finances small businesses, the equity that backs high-growth startups, the housing where employees live, and the big companies that are in the community (and are customers and partners for the small businesses) all depend on one another to be successful. A thriving ecosystem is not just a nice-to-have; it's a precondition for success.

In their book *The Rainforest*, Victor and his coauthor Greg Horowitt argue that humans don't think of great ideas alone: we have always been a collaborative species. The best solutions don't happen in isolation: the "rainforests" that yield the best ideas are environments where collaborators get input from a diversity of sources and species. The wrong way to find innovation, Hwang and Horowitt maintain, is to look for the next great idea; instead, investing in the right ecosystem creates an environment in which unexpected ideas can arise and thrive. Topophilia is one way to describe why an ecosystem works: people love and invest in where they are.

American history is full of stories of heroes who built ecosystems. In the 1950s, Ewing Marion Kauffman started a pharmaceutical company in Kansas City; he was proudest of the wealth he built for thousands of people in his hometown. Kauffman believed that the greatest virtue of entrepreneurship was being able to be self-reliant, and that if a person could do that, they would "not only be a better person, but a better productive citizen of the United States." Today, Victor Hwang leads entrepreneurship initiatives at the Kauffman Foundation, whose stated vision is "a society of economically independent individuals who are engaged citizens, contributing to the improvement of their communities."

I witnessed topophilia—love of place—in New Orleans, where we launched our first Village Capital investments. The entrepreneurs in New Orleans rallied together after Hurricane Katrina, and they often say that they care more about the success of New Orleans than they do about themselves. And in Louisville, Bryce Butler built Access Ventures as an ecosystem where people's money and community are interconnected: if you're an investor in Access Ventures, when you eat at Scarlet's Bakery, you know you are literally invested in its success, because you own an investment in the shop, and the employees live in real estate that you're also invested in.

Another type of ecosystem grows up within a particular sector. Matt Bannick and Paula Goldman of the Omidyar Network, the investment firm of eBay founder Pierre Omidyar, said in 2012, "Creating and scaling entire sectors can mean the difference between supporting one solar lantern company that can provide safe lights to thousands of people, and accelerating a solar lantern industry that can provide renewable, affordable power to millions."[104]

The microfinance industry that Bob Pattillo invested in has extended financial services to tens of millions of people, but it required an entire ecosystem. Bob made grants to the first microfinance industry association, helping create common standards for the industry: a tangible tool that ecosystem builders can learn from. (The common standards in successful industries such as microfinance are what inspired me and my team to create the VIRAL tool I described earlier.)

With a colleague, Genia Topple, he set up a group called Sanabel, which was the first microfinance association in the Middle East. And he set up multiple microfinance funds to invest in individual fund managers. Strong-functioning ecosystems invest in the human capacity for learning, giving individual innovators the time and space to create what's next. Today, thanks to investment from Bob Pattillo, Pierre Omidyar, and many others, there are thousands of microfinance banks around the world, and thousands more ideas given a chance to see the light. Village Capital is one output of these collaborations—remember our founding phrase: "If angel investing and microfinance had a baby."

If we want true innovation, focusing on heroes alone is not the way to get there. To solve the problem of innovation blind spots, we need to focus on the ecosystem these heroes are building around them. If you're a corporation, a foundation, or an individual that cares about innovation in a specific sector, whether it's global climate change or the renewal of manufacturing jobs in America, don't just look at specific firms. Look at the category of players who are setting industry standards, focusing on policy, and creating the pipeline for the next generation of innovators.

CHAPTER 13

"WE ARE THE THEY"

Building an Ecosystem

The invention of the spreadsheet screwed up a lot of things
for people. They think if I can't measure it, it has no value,
and nothing could be further from the truth. The most
valuable things can't be measured. And I'm not talking
about love, or air. I'm talking about innovation, ideas, and
culture.
> —Dan Gilbert, Founder and Chairman, Quicken
> Loans and Rock Ventures Family of Companies

The inches are everywhere. Every second counts: let's go!
> —Bruce Schwartz, Detroit Ambassador, Quicken
> Loans and Rock Ventures Family of Companies

We were standing on a freezing street corner in downtown Detroit in late January, and Bruce, our gregarious, smiling, porkpie hat–wearing tour guide, was urging us to jaywalk. We didn't see cars in either direction, so we ran across the street.

Bruce is the official Detroit ambassador for the Family of Companies, colloquially known as the FOC. And he's a Detroit institution: if you walk down the street with Bruce, every third person enthusiastically greets him by name.

A decade ago, not many people were walking down the main streets of Detroit at all, let alone for a tour. But in the last few years, the city has seen an impressive resurgence. Unemployment has decreased from 28 percent to 6 percent, and there's been a 73 percent growth in new startups. And the FOC is perhaps the largest reason why.

The FOC encompasses more than one hundred companies, from major market player Quicken Loans to the Cleveland Cavaliers to Bedrock, the largest private real estate investor in Detroit. Collectively, the FOC has invested over $2 billion in rebuilding Detroit and Cleveland. Entrepreneur Dan Gilbert, born and raised in Detroit, is the owner and chairman of the FOC, and he views everything he's doing as integrated in one pocket.

Nathaniel Hawthorne wrote that "families are always rising and falling in America." I think the same can be said of communities. Today, Silicon Valley is the envy of the world, but fifty years ago, the area was nothing but apple orchards. Fifty years ago, the Motor City was the wealthiest community in the country; in 2013 the city went bankrupt. But Detroit isn't dead—and Dan Gilbert's family of companies is perhaps the biggest reason why. Detroit is coming back because it's working as an ecosystem rather than a collection of firms.

In 2008, over half of Detroit's downtown buildings were unoccupied. No one on the Quicken Loans team worked downtown. After the Great Recession, Dan decided that Quicken and Detroit would rise together and made all employees of the FOC relocate from the Detroit suburbs. By 2016, Quicken's FOC alone had over seventeen thousand employees in Detroit, and the rest of the FOC had thousands more. Quicken is now Detroit's largest employer and its largest minority employer. The company is best in its class, ranked number one by J. D. Power in customer satisfaction for mortgage origination and customer experience. And the ripple effects are spreading. Today, Detroit's office space is at capacity: when Microsoft wanted to move into downtown Detroit, they couldn't even find office space until Dan volunteered to move an entire floor of Quicken Loans elsewhere.

The FOC team members believe in the ecosystem. They are known for their "ISMs"—quirky, memorable mantras that define the values across the specific companies. One of my favorites is "We are the 'they.'" On my tour of Detroit, after Bruce and I ran across the street, he pointed out a beautiful Art Deco bus station that Bedrock had recently purchased. He noticed that the time on the clock wasn't right, so he quickly texted a colleague at Bedrock, the FOC's full-service real estate arm, to let them know. "I didn't want to just say, 'They should fix it,'" Bruce said. "We are the 'they.' I don't work for Bedrock, but we're all working for a larger impact. If you come to Detroit and see a clock that isn't running on time, you might leave thinking a little bit less of the city."

Quicken Loans has been named J. D. Power's "Best Place to Work" seven years in a row, and one-pocket thinking is likely the biggest reason why. As I walked the loan origination floor at Quicken Loans, with twenty-three-year-old recent graduates of Wayne State calling people to offer lower interest rates on their mortgage, and as I spoke with the security guards at the front desks of Bedrock's properties, I asked what they liked most about their job. "The impact," everyone said. "We're building something bigger than ourselves."

Dan describes the FOC ecosystem this way: "We never look at a business decision the way normal people would look at it, and say, 'Does this piece of real estate or does this investment have the opportunity to become income-producing?' Instead, we look at each investment as a piece of the puzzle and evaluate how it will fit."

As one example, one of the FOC's large investments was in an Internet access company. In 2015, three employees of Quicken Loans, Marc Hudson, Edi Demaj, and Randy Foster, were working on new interfaces to automate loan pricing and make loans faster. They realized that Detroit's Internet speed was one of the rate limiters to Quicken's success. They developed an idea for a faster fiber optic, and quickly developed a separate company. Now, when you walk the streets of Detroit with Bruce, he'll point out where they've dug up the concrete to lay high-speed fiber optic across the city. Dan proudly points out that Detroit has the fastest Internet in America. The FOC didn't set out to invest in a Rocket Fiber primarily because they thought the firm would be successful, or because they wanted to invest in an Internet company. They saw an investment opportunity that would power the entire ecosystem.

SUCCESSFUL ECOSYSTEMS ARE ABOUT MORE THAN PROFIT

Successful ecosystems create one-pocket thinkers in the process. "I hate the phrases 'nonprofit' and 'for-profit,'" says Dan. "I think of what we do as more-than-profit. People have a hard time understanding that when you do more than profit, you also make more profit. Not only are people here impacting things, they're better at their day job because they're impacting things."

Detroit became the wealthiest city in the country in the 1960s because a previous civic leader, Henry Ford, thought similarly. "When Henry Ford started his company," says Dan, "he didn't even have the workers here. He had to go to the South and pitch the workers to come. He offered five dollars a day, which was an outrageous amount of money." But as Dan likes to remind people, every Ford worker could buy a car.

Dan doesn't encourage people to try to replicate what he's doing in Detroit. He knows that what works for Detroit wouldn't work for St. Louis or Louisville. Instead of copying and pasting, he wants people across the country to develop their own one-pocket, more-than-profit way to build profitable and successful ecosystems. When I visited Dan, he had just spent the weekend with Kevin Plank, CEO of Under Armour, who is playing a leading role in the future of Baltimore. Dan hopes that Kevin, and hundreds more like him, will succeed in building great businesses and great communities. "Wouldn't it be nice in this country," Dan says, "if we could show people a lot more examples of more-than-profit? Then they'd believe, as a body of work, that you could do this."

BEING A PART OF THE BODY OF WORK

Whether you're a business leader, a politician, a philanthropist, or—especially—a regular community member, you can play a role in building that body of work. You can be the leader who helps build the ecosystem.

One great playbook for how to create an ecosystem in your hometown is Techstars founder Brad Feld's book *Startup Communities*. He highlights a theory of ecosystem building that he calls the "Boulder thesis," after one of the leaders in topophilia that Colorado governor John Hickenlooper cited. Brad and his colleagues have been able to inspire dozens of people across Colorado to build ecosystem-enabling organizations. If you're an entrepreneur trying to start a technology company in Boulder, the ecosystem has ways to support you at every step of the journey:

- If you've got an idea that you want to turn into a company, you can attend a Startup Weekend, funded by grants from Brad and other entrepreneurs and investors in the ecosystem.
- If you feel you're underrepresented—a victim of the "leaky pipeline"—you can take advantage of the Techstars Foundation, funded by grants from people looking to build a recruitment pipeline.
- If you've launched your company and are looking for customers, funding, and people who can help, you can go through Brad's accelerator Techstars, funded by angel investors.

- If you're growing, you can raise money from Brad's venture firm, Foundry Group, funded by the types of people who are interested in traditional venture funds.

Brad and his colleagues stress that they are more interested in the success of Boulder as a community than in any specific investment they make—indeed, they've invested more in Boulder's success than in any specific firm. And their ecosystem investments have paid off: Boulder now has six times the startups per capita of the average city in America, and twice as many as Silicon Valley.[105]

When you invest at an ecosystem level—not just picking and choosing specific firms—you make true change. Today, I see venture firms that say, "We'd love to invest in more women and people of color—we just have a pipeline problem." As Freada Kapor Klein says, "Certainly, that is true: the pool of female candidates starting a big technology platform is smaller than that of men. But long before those career paths start, I see the long journey of the hidden biases and barriers that keep all of us on different paths in our lives. This includes everything from access to broadband, role models, and even the unspoken messages of social belonging and peer acceptance."

Investing in an ecosystem improves the pool of candidates for founders, early employees, and future angel investors. Investing in an ecosystem is less tangible than throwing your money and support behind one entrepreneur. But it's planting a forest you'll harvest over time, and remember: the second-best time to plant a tree is now.

ENSURE YOU'RE NOT TRYING TO IMPOSE A "ONE SIZE FITS ALL" ECOSYSTEM ON YOUR COMMUNITY

As you think about how you can develop your own ecosystem, make sure that what you do works for you. Investing in an ecosystem requires a hard look at structures that are unique to—and that work for—a specific community, rather than replicating the blind spots of other ecosystems.

Silicon Valley thrives because it's a great ecosystem. If you're in the right networks, you're able to connect with anyone. But very often, I've seen well-intentioned ecosystem development efforts fall short by trying to clone others rather than embracing what makes their place unique. The way we will close innovation blind spots is not by copying and pasting what works in Silicon Valley; it's through creating what Jim Fallows calls "archipelagos of start-ups and reinventions."

Detroit has its own future, with strengths in financial services and transportation. New Orleans has promise in education technology and food. Chicago, Durham, Omaha, Nairobi, Hyderabad, and Mexico City each has its own strengths. When you try to transplant the Silicon Valley model into another ecosystem, the city often rejects it, like an organ donor recipient rejecting a kidney. Dan Gilbert believes this. "People always ask me, 'Are you trying to be the next Silicon Valley?' No! You can't. I want to be the next Detroit."

One model that works great in some instances, but can be too one-size-fits-all for others, is the accelerator, as popularized by the likes of YCombinator and Techstars. Cities and corporations have adopted the accelerator model worldwide—the Kauffman Foundation estimates that there are over 650 accelerators around the world. The most common version of an accelerator program will recruit ten founders to one shared working space and provide them with three months of mentorship and support—and possibly cash—in exchange for equity. But if you're asking an entrepreneur to move to a specific location for a three-month program, you're seriously restricting the pipeline of who can be involved: for example, founders with families to take care of often can't move to a new location. The accelerator model also ignores the many people in the ecosystem who don't have their own startup—perhaps they don't have $30,000 to start a company, or they can't afford to leave behind the health insurance and other benefits they get from working at a larger company.

Physical spaces for entrepreneurs have also arisen around the world, with a business model of real estate—renting out seats and offering programming for companies. Yet the evidence is mixed on whether these real estate companies, which are often pressed to monetize from cash-strapped innovations quickly, deliver better companies in the short term.

An accelerator and/or a coworking space could be a critical part of an ecosystem investment strategy, but if you're truly investing in an ecosystem, you need to develop the right solution for the right problem. Is access to capital a problem? Figure out a strategy to get new capital to founders that isn't just an accelerator program. And figure out why founders need capital. If hardware entrepreneurs need it to build their inventions, maybe you can support lab space. If a disproportionate number of your founders are from low-wealth backgrounds and don't have friends and family with money, maybe you can build a grant facility to support the $30,000 in start-up costs that the Kauffman Foundation estimates it takes to start a company.

Another model that doesn't fit is an attempt to raise as much venture capital as possible. Venture capital firms are incentivized to provide as high a return as possible in as short a time as possible—indeed, the average venture capital firm's dream would be an IPO or an acquisition from a major player. But these are often limiting factors. Dan Gilbert would have a much harder time building an ecosystem in Detroit if he were a public company, since he makes investments and buys companies and properties that will have value over decades but would be hard to show the value of in the next quarter. Kim Jordan says that if New Belgium had raised venture capital investment, 100 percent employee ownership would be nearly impossible to achieve because Anheuser-Busch InBev, the global brewing conglomerate, could always offer a higher price for acquisition than her employees. Kim and Dan believe that they will ultimately derive more value from what they have.

Venture capital is a great fit in the right place and time. America Online was able to ultimately help Steve Case seed Rise of the Rest, and they raised venture capital, as have most of the great enterprises mentioned in this book. But just as accelerators can't be a "one size fits all" solution, neither can venture capital. From revenue sharing to employee stock ownership plans, I look forward to innovation in a broad range of tools that can seed our innovators.

THE BEST NEWS: ONE ECOSYSTEM SUCCESS CAN YIELD CHILDREN AND GRANDCHILDREN

If you're feeling less than hopeful about your place and community, keep in mind that a small success can change the ecosystem. Quicken Loans' success in changing how people got mortgages over the Internet led to an entire family of companies that revitalized Detroit. Similarly, when Michael Dell started the business that would ultimately become Dell Technologies in his dorm room in Austin, Texas, he created a generation of "Dellionaires" that have fueled a revival of Austin. We're seeing similar resurgence in Baltimore thanks to Under Armour's success.

Jean Case, CEO of the Case Foundation, has helped change a two-pocket conversation in philanthropy to a one-pocket one. Jean has been a leader in the impact investing movement, cochairing the US National Advisory Board on Impact Investing, which pioneered policies that better blend business and purpose. The Case Foundation also launched the Startup America Partnership after the Great Recession, an initiative to promote startup success everywhere, in an effort to contribute to the body of work of ecosystem leaders across the United States. And as Chairman of the National Geographic Society, she has led the board to turn a nonprofit that's over 125 years old into a one-pocket organization that is beginning to invest its endowment in businesses that are aligned with the organization's goals.

An Internet switchboard in Dulles, Virginia, generated a boom of Internet companies and a thriving startup ecosystem; nearly every important startup in the DC area over the past twenty years can trace its success in some way to AOL. In 2005, Steve Case joined forces with Donn Davis and Tige Savage, two team members from AOL, to create Revolution. Their mission was to make investments that would transform old industries. In transportation, for example, Revolution was the first major investor in Zipcar—creating the category of ride-sharing and paving the way for Uber, Lyft, and a generation change in transportation. In food, Revolution has backed Revolution Foods, Sweetgreen, Cava, and a host of startups in DC and beyond that have turned cafeteria food and fast food into healthier choices for the population. Revolution now manages over $1 billion to invest in real-world industries—with a specific focus on industries outside New York, Boston, and San Francisco.

Ted Leonsis became president and vice chairman of AOL in 1994. Ted now owns the Verizon Center, the Washington Wizards, and the Washington Capitals, and as a result he is one of the largest employers in the region. He is also a partner in Revolution's growth fund.

Blackboard, a DC-based company whose learning management system is in 75 percent of universities and 50 percent of K–12 schools in the United States, received early venture investment from AOL. And 1776 is a global coworking space and investment fund that actively invests in one-pocket companies—also with a great deal of help from early AOL team members. Village Capital is based in Washington, DC; our investment fund has significant backing from Jean and Steve Case, as well as other early AOL team members.

On a spreadsheet, you can measure what it costs to invest in an ecosystem but not necessarily what it's worth. But if we are going to close innovation blind spots, we need to ensure that the best ideas connect with the people who have resources, regardless of where they come from. No one firm or hero can do that. But a thriving ecosystem, one that produces an army of heroes, can.

CHAPTER 14

WHAT CAN HAPPEN TO THE AMERICAN DREAM?

No man can be a good citizen unless he has a wage more than sufficient to cover the bare cost of living, and hours of labor short enough so after his day's work is done he will have time and energy to bear his share in the management of the community, to help in carrying the general load. We keep countless men from being good citizens by the conditions of life by which we surround them.
—Theodore Roosevelt

People don't write books because they've got a great deal of wisdom to impart to somebody; they write books because they want to find the answers for themselves and share the search. It's not "I have a thing to tell you," even if you say it is. It's an exploration and a discovery.
—Shelby Foote

Let's return to the question that opened the first chapter: What happened to the American Dream? Just as I began this book using entrepreneurship as a lens through which we can understand today's economy, I'd like to end it using the American Dream as a lens through which we can understand the economy's future.

When I'm traveling to rural areas that we invest in, I sometimes stop in at the local McDonald's, which photojournalist Chris Arnade calls "the glue that holds communities together." I was once at a McDonald's about forty-five minutes from Charlottesville, Virginia, in a town called Orange, population 4,700. I sat down with my coffee and started talking with five regulars seated at a semicircular table, each with a one-dollar, unlimited-refill coffee, and over our hour-long conversation, another fifteen regulars dropped in and out of the conversation.

The folks in Orange asked what I did for a living, and when I explained, they said, "Small business is our only hope here." They pointed to a nearly deserted clapboard Main Street and said, "We used to have the hardware store there; when they opened the Lowe's twenty miles away, well, that went under. The Walmart in Locust Grove killed off a few more businesses. Now, McDonald's is all we have."

Our heads-down drive for progress has hollowed out many communities. The thinking behind Peter Thiel's maxim for entrepreneurs—"Be a monopoly"—has caused a lot of people to lose their livelihoods and their dreams. Stockholders in Walmart, Lowe's, Home Depot, McDonald's, and Amazon push growth at all costs; meanwhile, these big-box stores cut prices on their most competitive goods to eliminate any local competition. My grandfather remembers when his immigrant Croatian father had to deal with the effect of a changing economy on his hardware store in Gary, Indiana: "When the big-box hardware store opened nearby," he says, "we felt it immediately."

Barry Lynn, Matt Stoller, Philip Longman, and others have written extensively on monopoly thinking and the resulting concentration in colossal companies. They argue that monopolies have had a destructive effect on our economy's vitality. As an example, 62 percent of the black-owned banks that were in operation in 1980 are now gone, and 96 percent of the black-owned insurance companies in the United States have gone out of business in the last forty years. Why? Big-company concentration. As Brian Feldman writes, "As large retailers and financial institutions comprise an ever-bigger slice of the national economy, the possibility of starting and maintaining an independent business has dropped."[106] Matt Stoller provides a body of evidence that monopoly power has been more destructive for jobs than trade deals or automation: he estimates that the concentration of economic activities in big companies has cost the average worker $14,000 a year in take-home pay over the past thirty years.[107]

I asked Larry, one of the men in Orange, what he would do if he had the financing to start a business. He said, "I'd start a coffee shop. We sit here every day, in these crappy chairs, drinking our coffee, and sending our money halfway across the country. I'd rather send money to someone I know, and have the place I'm buying coffee give a damn about how good the chairs are."

For roughly four decades, big business has held sway in American politics, tilting laws and rules to promote concentration. Today, Walmart has disaster recovery centers, crime prevention policies, and a foreign policy apparatus. It's looking more like a central-planned government than the free enterprise it was intended to be. And the freedom of would-be entrepreneurs like Larry to even try to follow their dreams is taken away. This isn't just a Walmart problem: large platforms like Google, Amazon, and Facebook have had the same chilling effect on everything from retail to news.

The problem: when large conglomerates touch every part of everyday life, local problems are harder to solve. Today Walmart executives in Bentonville, Arkansas, and Facebook leadership in Palo Alto make centralized decisions about highly sensitive local problems, and we have fewer local leaders with an independent base and the knowledge of our communities' problems needed to be able to solve them. As Justice Louis Brandeis once warned, we are becoming a nation of clerks.

Corporations have never been bigger and the Dow Jones is at an all-time high, but all too many people are sitting in a McDonald's, drinking coffee, wondering where their town went, shifting uncomfortably in their chairs.

MONOPOLY VS. TOPOPHILIA

What does this all have to do with blind spots?

I started writing this book because I wanted to understand a problem. It seems obvious to me that our innovation blind spots are making all our other problems more difficult to solve. "One size fits all" means that the coffee shop that Larry wants to start in Orange, Virginia, doesn't fit any investor's patterns. The "Big Sort" means that a Harvard MBA living in New York and working for McKinsey is likely advising Lowe's on how to price its products so that it can put the hardware store on Main Street in Orange out of business as quickly as possible. And "It's not what you know; it's who you know" means that Larry's grandkids in rural Orange probably won't have the chance to sit in the same seat that the Harvard MBA does.

The fundamental debate we have today is not right versus left or business versus nonprofit. It's monopoly versus topophilia. Conglomerate versus community. "Davos Man"—the suit-wearing Master of the Universe who gathers at the annual Davos summit in Switzerland to discuss the fate of the world—versus entrepreneur. Top-down versus bottom-up. "Too big to fail" versus "too small to succeed."

And big institutions don't necessarily need to be the enemy—they just need to not be "too big to fail." Google and Facebook will have better news and content and more relevant ads if they empower, rather than crowd out, local content producers. Banks, venture capital firms, and financial services institutions need to figure out how to invest at the topophilia level if they are going to get truly different, interesting, and profitable ideas. For our innovation economy to succeed in creating a better future, we need to create conditions where everyone is able to play in the innovation game.

We need to create the conditions where people like Larry (or Laura) at least have the chance to try and build that coffee shop.

The new social contract should be: if you've got a great idea, no matter who you are or where you live, you'll have the chance at least to *try*. Not necessarily to succeed, or even reach equality of outcomes. But the right, in the words of Ewing Kauffman, an entrepreneur who built a billion-dollar company in Kansas City in the twentieth century, "to take the calculated risk, to dream, to build, yes, even to fail, and to succeed."

AN UNWINDING AND A REAWAKENING

At the beginning of this book I mentioned George Packer's theory about the slow "unwinding" of the American Dream. Packer points out, though, that this isn't the first time this has happened. The American Revolution was an "unwinding," but it turned a loose confederation of states into the United States of America. The Great Depression and World War II gave way to the Greatest Generation. As Packer writes, "Each decline brought renewal; each implosion released energy; out of each unwinding brought new cohesion."

I am hopeful that today's economic devastation can provide fresh opportunity to close our blind spots and, specifically, turn our "too big to fail" innovation industrial complex into a "small enough to succeed" democracy of ideas. We need new ideas, we need a lot of them, we need them locally, and we need them quickly. But we're not going to fix the problems we have by trying to replicate what's working in places like Silicon Valley and then becoming patrons of the rest of world through a universal government-backed basic income.

If you're grinding it out every day where you live, this book hopes to show you that you're not alone; you're part of a larger body of work. The CEOs we should admire are people like Kim Jordan, who built a company based on the way she wanted to live her life, and gave all employees secure retirement in the process.

They're people like Ewing Kauffman, who cared more about the wealth he was building for Kansas City than the wealth he built for himself, and believed that being a better person and being a better citizen are the same thing. They're people like Lula Luu, who could live anywhere but chose to build a company in Paducah, Kentucky, providing meaning and purpose for her team members. And they're people like Dan Gilbert, who brought together over a hundred disparate companies into a tight-knit family and believes they will be successful only when their community is successful.

The pioneers I see are Jerry Nemorin, moving across the country to California not in a gold rush for himself but to raise money to help people like his mom get out of debt. And they're people like Clarence Bethea and Jewel Burks, who quit their jobs to start a new company because they saw a better idea that no one else saw.

The heroes in government making the biggest difference are at the local level, not the federal. I see Republicans like Ashley Swearengin in California and Richard Berry in New Mexico, and Democrats like Greg Fischer in Kentucky and Stacey Abrams in Georgia, as leaders who are able to earn bipartisan respect and make tangible progress in their communities. And our modern-day folk heroes are people like Steve Case, who is riding across the country on a bus, like a twenty-first-century Johnny Appleseed, planting what will become the foundation of Rise of the Rest with investments in ecosystems.

The people in this book aren't examples to copy and paste; they're fellow travelers. The answer for any city's future is not "Do exactly what Dan Gilbert has done in Detroit." It's "Take what the ecosystem leaders in this book have done as an inspiration, and become a place where the entrepreneurs feel welcome and want to live." And add your own spin, depending on what matters in your own place.

In a podcast shortly after releasing his book, George Packer reflected on the opportunity to build on this moment and change the way we organize our American economy: Do we change the system, and then hope that people's values change? Or do we change people's values, and then hope that the system changes to match?

It's a fundamental question. Someone like Karl Marx or Ayn Rand would start with the system: create a fully socialist or fully libertarian society, and values will adapt. The flip side is the moralist tradition, best captured by Charles Dickens: change Ebenezer Scrooge's heart and he'll give Bob Cratchit a raise, and spare Tiny Tim from dying in poverty.

But I think the question assumes a false choice. The economic decisions we make are composed of values plus information. But in a big-data world where we are pushing to maximize quarterly earnings and focusing on the most perfect information possible, we have lost sight of the values we care about. We prioritize the quarterly share price of Lowe's, Walmart, and Home Depot and then later worry about the social fabric of Orange, Virginia, but we don't recognize that they are interconnected. We can't price the long-term social and environmental risks that we create with a two-pocket world, so we don't value them.

The new social contract, giving people the freedom to try, is the best answer I've found to change this. We most value who and what we know, so we need to start with our communities. And we need to give people the chance to start small, and the opportunity (but not the requirement) to build big. This book is about entrepreneurship, but topophilia can mean anything from local newspapers to craft beer to, yes, the next great startup idea.

What can happen to the American Dream? Let's not try and restore it through a few large cartels, cities, firms, and investment strategies. The United States of America has succeeded over the past 250 years because, at its founding, it had the most educated population in the world, the highest literacy rate among women, and the lowest poverty rate, and the unparalleled economic prosperity of the twentieth century happened because we had the highest rate of entrepreneurship and education worldwide. All these ideas happened from the bottom up. Locally organized schools and religious institutions educated early Americans. The idea of universal high school was not a federal mandate; it was a few innovators in Iowa whose ideas spread nationally.

My hope is that this book provides a blueprint for an innovation economy that is bottom-up, not top-down. To succeed, we need to make the weakest link as strong as possible rather than search for a few heroes at the top. And if you're inspired to close blind spots, I hope I've given you a few places to start.

As the quotation from Shelby Foote suggests, I didn't start Village Capital—or write this book—because I think I know all the answers to what's wrong. I do know that the system isn't working, and I hope that my career—and now this book—can help me figure out how to make things better. I'm eager for your thoughts as we go along the journey together.

ACKNOWLEDGMENTS

One of the great lessons of *The Innovation Blind Spot* is that we thrive in community, and writing this book has made me very grateful for the community of brilliant, thoughtful, and supportive people I am lucky enough to be a part of.

First of all, I'm grateful for the many people who read and edited drafts, and who walked through the journey of writing with me. Ben Wrobel has an uncanny knack for what people actually care about, and is one of the most gifted writers I've ever worked with. Connor Sullivan understands that all times are one time and pushed me to turn individual ideas into truths that resonate widely. Davis Zaunbrecher traveled with me on thousands of miles of road, collecting many of the early stories that helped me build this book. Andrew Simmons delivered feedback that I was crying out for—feedback that was needed, and needed badly. Writing a book is a distinct skill set, not a mystery: thanks to Adam Grant for teaching me this. Jennifer Lee helped me figure out what a book is for. Frank Gruber provided valuable insights on the writing and marketing process. Ann DeRosa helped me see ten years into the future, casting a vision for what a new economy could look like that we are all filling in. Michael Anne Kyle was my toughest customer: when she liked something, I knew it was good. (I also cut a whole chapter because of her.) Robbie Brown has never been afraid to try anything in his life and has a nose for a good story. And Herbie Ziskend helped me "get it," and made the entire process fun.

As I said in the book, in the words of Shelby Foote, you don't write a book because you have something to say. You write a book because you want to learn something and share the journey. I'm most grateful to the entrepreneurs in the book for sharing their stories. Kim Jordan, Clarence Bethea, Tony Aguilar, Herbert Moore, Vicki Zhou, Lula Luu, John Crilly, Yvette Ondachi, Myles Lutheran, Marion Moon, Jerry Nemorin, and dozens more have inspired my thinking in this book and helped me to see the world differently. And to the original entrepreneur and Inkler, Bob Pattillo, I'm grateful for the chance to even do this work. You guys are the reason all this work matters.

I'm also grateful to the people I shared the journey with. Many of them shared their stories with me, and you can learn about them in the book. Thanks to Steve Case for inviting me on the bus, and on the road, to discover great ideas around the world hiding in plain sight, and to Jean Case, for teaching me how to be fearless in so many ways. Dane Stangler helped me create the intellectual architecture for this book's argument and find the data behind the stories, and he helped crystallize a lot of these ideas. A huge thank you to the team at the Kauffman Foundation, specifically Wendy Guillies and Victor Hwang, who helped me find clarity in how to message the big picture and understand how to make this more broadly relevant. Brian Trelstad helped me understand where this story fit in the big picture of the capital markets. Justin Berg gave me useful insights on forecasting and how to be a "super-forecaster." John Lettieri and Steve Glickman helped me understand the decline of American dynamism. Matt Stoller helped me understand competition policy and how to unwind the concentration. And Daniel Hemel checked and challenged every assumption I made, ensuring a more intellectually honest argument in the process.

Many of the thoughts in this book are collective. Bryce Butler, Graham Macmillan, and Kelly Michel taught me what topophilia really means and why you should invest in ecosystems, not just firms. Sheila Herrling has the unique skill of being your toughest critic and biggest fan in the same sentence. David Kyle offered me a job on a phone call that had the description of "Come help out" in India, and the rest of the ride has been unforgettable. Dan Gilbert, Andrea English, and Bruce Schwartz gave me an unforgettable day in Detroit, where the inches were everywhere. Josh Woodward is a paragon of everything that's right with Silicon Valley and helped me bridge the two worlds. PG Sittenfeld is an example of everything that's right with Cincinnati and can help translate where our cities are going. Many thanks to Brad Feld for helping me realize a way to do venture capital that works—it looks a lot like topophilia. I've traveled a circuit with Simon Desjardins, Paul Breloff, and Lauren Cochran, and a lot of these arguments were developed over awesome late-night sessions with them. Mitch Kapor, Freada Kapor Klein, and Ben Jealous have illuminated many of my blind spots and made me stronger in the process. Finally, Katelyn Donnelly, Caitlyn Fox, and Kevin Jones helped me think through and articulate the combination of what we do and why we do it: "two-pocket thinking."

My team at Village Capital, most of all, has inspired, sustained, and grown the ideas in this book. Victoria Fram, my cofounder, is the most capable person I will ever work with. Allie Burns taught me that vision without execution is hallucination. Dahler Battle was the tip of the spear on this book, helping me get the first draft on paper. Many thanks to my teammates who read drafts, provided feedback, and have worked with me along the way, including Chris Cusack, Aaron Coleman, Lia Mayka, Nasir Qadree, Jared Marquette, Heather Strachan, Ebony Pope, Michele Rivard, Greg Bennett, Andrew Hobbs, Ben Younkman, Bidisha Bhattacharyya, Amanda Jacobson, Dustin Shay, and Daniel Hsu.

I'd also like to thank Michael Harriot for guiding me through the process of finding a publisher, and Leah Wilson, Laurel Leigh, Glenn Yeffeth, and the whole amazing team at BenBella books for their support and fantastic partnership. In a world where bigger isn't always better, I felt like the most important person in the world at all times to the whole BenBella and Folio team.

Finally, I'd like to thank my family: my mom, who gave me the original time and space and companionship to get this first draft down on paper in Richmond; my grandfather, one of the original Illuminators; and Jen, who is responsible for cutting everything devastating from the book, making it much funnier, and inspiring the title. And certainly not least of all, Greg, the ultimate companion during the writing process, even if unaware I was writing a book at all.

NOTES

1. Taleb, Nassim Nicholas. *The Bed of Procrustes: Philosophical and Practical Aphorisms*. New York: Random House, 2010. Print.
2. "The University Entrepreneurship Report: Alumni of Top Universities Rake in $12.6 Billion Across 559 Deals." *CB Insights*. N.p., October 31, 2012. Web. January 4, 2017. <http://www.cbinsights.com/blog/venture-capital/university-entrepreneurship-report>
3. Wilson, Mark. "This $1,500 Toaster Oven Is Everything That's Wrong With Silicon Valley Design." *Co.Design*. N.p., December 2, 2016. Web. January 4, 2017. <https://www.fastcodesign.com/3065667/this-1500-toaster-oven-is-everything-thats-wrong-with-silicon-valley-design>
4. Kane, Tim. "The Importance of Startups in Job Creation and Job Destruction." *The Ewing Marion Kauffman Foundation*, July 2010. <http://www.kauffman.org/~/media/kauffman_org/research%20reports%20and%20covers/2010/07/firm_formation_importance_of_startups.pdf>
5. Motoyama, Yasuyuki, and Jason Wiens. "Guidelines for Local and State Governments to Promote Entrepreneurship." *The Ewing Marion Kauffman Foundation*, March 10, 2015. <http://www.kauffman.org/what-we-do/research/2015/03/guidelines-for-local-and-state-governments-to-promote-entrepreneurship>
6. Hathaway, Ian, Jordan Bell-Masterson, and Dane Stangler. "New Business Creation." *Kauffman Foundation Research Series* (2013): n. pag. Kauffman Foundation, July 2013. Web. December 2, 2015. <http://www.kauffman.org/~/media/kauffman_org/research%20reports%20and%20covers/2013/07/firmformationandeconomicgrowthjuly2013.pdf>
7. "Dynamism in Retreat: Consequences for Regions, Markets, and Workers." *Economic Innovation Group* (2017): *www.eig.com*. Economic Innovation Group, February 2017. Web. February 3, 2017. <http://eig.org/wp-content/uploads/2017/02/Dynamism-in-Retreat.pdf>

8. Fikri, Kenan. "Dynamism in Retreat." *Economic Innovation Group,* February 2017. Web. March 21, 2017. <http://eig.org/wp-content /uploads/2017/02/Dynamism-in-Retreat.pdf>

9. Fikri, Kenan. "Dynamism in Retreat." *Economic Innovation Group,* February 2017. Web. March 21, 2017. <http://eig.org/wp-content /uploads/2017/02/Dynamism-in-Retreat.pdf>

10. Gillespie, Patrick. "Americans Are Saving More Than Spending." *CNN Money.* CNN, November 25, 2015. Web. December 3, 2015; Said, Carolyn. "Bootstrapped Startups Buck Trend Toward VC Bucks." *San Francisco Chronicle,* August 8, 2015. Web. October 22, 2015; Gabler, Neal. "The Secret Shame of Middle-Class Americans." *The Atlantic.* Atlantic Media Company, May 2016. Web. February 3, 2017. <http:// www.theatlantic.com/magazine/archive/2016/05/my-secret-shame /476415/>

11. Blanco, Octavio. "Why So Few Latino-Owned Businesses Get Venture Capital Funding." *CNNMoney.* Cable News Network, April 12, 2016. Web. January 3, 2017. http://money.cnn.com/2016/04/12/smallbusiness /latino-venture-capital/; Meisler, Laura, Mira Rojanasakul, and Jeremy Scott Diamond. "Who Gets Venture Capital Funding?" Bloomberg. com. Bloomberg, May 25, 2016. Web. December 20, 2016. <https:// www.bloomberg.com/graphics/2016-who-gets-vc-funding/>

12. "Interview with Jerry Nemorin." Personal interview. July 27, 2016.

13. PwC. "PwC/CB Insights MoneyTree Report Q1 2017/" *PwC,* January 2017. Web. April 13 2017. < https://www.pwc.com/us/en/technology /moneytree.html>

14. Nicholas, Tom, and Jonas Peter Akins. "Whaling Ventures." *Harvard Business School Case 813-086,* October 2012. Revised March 2016.

15. "Fin-tech." *The Economist.* The Economist Newspaper, January 2, 2016. Web. February 3, 2017. <http://www.economist.com/news/finance -and-economics/21684805-there-were-tech-startups-there-was -whaling-fin-tech>

16. Mulcahy, Diane. "Venture Capitalists Get Paid Well to Lose Money." *Harvard Business Review,* August 5, 2014. Web. December 20, 2016. <https://hbr.org/2014/08/venture-capitalists-get-paid-well-to -lose-money>

17. Rhodes-Kropf, Matthew, Josh Lerner, and Ann Leamon. "Iris Running Crane: December 2009." *Harvard Business School Case 810-073,* December 2009. (Revised July 2013.)

18. World Economic Forum (WEF) Investors Industries, in collaboration with Deloitte Touche Tohmatsu, *From the Margins to the Mainstream: Assessment of the Impact Investment Sector and Opportunities to Engage Mainstream Investors.* September 2013.

19. Cutler, Kim-Mai. "Lessons from a Study of Perfect Pitch Decks: VCs Spend an Average of 3 Minutes, 44 Seconds on Them." *TechCrunch.* DocSend, June 8, 2015. Web. December 20, 2016. <https://techcrunch.com/2015/06/08/lessons-from-a-study-of-perfect-pitch-decks-vcs-spend-an-average-of-3-minutes-44-seconds-on-them/>

20. Gigerenzer, Gerd, and Daniel G. Goldstein. "Reasoning the fast and frugal way: models of bounded rationality." *Psychological review* 103.4 (1996): 650.

21. Newman, Kira. "The 25 Top VC Firms." *Tech.Co.* N.p., February 26, 2015. Web. February 3, 2017. <http://tech.co/top-vc-firms-to-pitch-your-startup-to-2015-02>

22. Fairlie, Robert W., and Alicia M. Robb. *Race and Entrepreneurial Success: Black-, Asian-, and White-Owned Businesses in the United States.* Cambridge, MA: MIT, 2008. Print.

23. Mulcahy, Diane, Bill Weeks, and Harold S. Bradley. *We Have Met the Enemy and He Is Us.* Rep. Kansas City: Kauffman Foundation, 2012. Print.

24. Wilson, Fred. "AVC." *VC Fund Economics—AVC.* Union Square Ventures, May 13, 2014. Web. February 3, 2017. <http://avc.com/2014/05/vc-fund-economics/>

25. Johnson, Carolyn Y. "The Wildly Hyped $9 Billion Blood Test Company That No One Really Understands." *The Washington Post.* WP, October 15, 2015. Web. February 3, 2017. <https://www.washingtonpost.com/news/wonk/wp/2015/10/15/the-wildly-hyped-9-billion-blood-test-company-that-no-one-really-understands/?utm_term=.878a5baee488>

26. Abelson, Reed. "Theranos to Close Labs and Lay Off 340 Workers." *The New York Times.* The New York Times, October 5, 2016. Web. February 3, 2017. <https://www.nytimes.com/2016/10/06/business/theranos-to-close-labs-and-lay-off-340-workers.html?_r=0>

27. Kelly, Donna, Abdul Ali, Candida Brush, Andrew Corbett, Caroline Daniels, Phillip Kim, Thomas Lyons, Mahdi Majbouri, and Edward Rogoff. "United States." *Global Entrepreneurship Monitor* (2014): n. pag. Babson College, 2015. Web. October 20, 2015.

28. Fry, Richard. "The Changing Profile of Student Borrowers." *Pew Research Centers Social Demographic Trends Project RSS*. Pew Research, October 7, 2014. Web. October 22, 2015; Looney, Adam, and Constantine Yannelis. "A Crisis in Student Loans?: How Changes in the Characteristics of Borrowers and in the Institutions They Attended Contributed to Rising Loan Defaults." *Brookings Papers on Economic Activity* 2015.2 (2015): 1-89. Brookings, September 10, 2015. Web. February 3, 2017. <http://www.brookings.edu/~/media/projects/bpea /fall-2015_embargoed/conferencedraft_looneyyannelis_student loandefaults.pdf>

29. Looney, Adam, and Constantine Yannelis. "A Crisis in Student Loans?: How Changes in the Characteristics of Borrowers and in the Institutions They Attended Contributed to Rising Loan Defaults." *Brookings Papers on Economic Activity* 2015.2 (2015): 1-89. Brookings, September 10, 2015. Web. February 3, 2017. <http://www.brookings.edu/~/media /projects/bpea/fall-2015_embargoed/conferencedraft_looney yannelis_studentloandefaults.pdf>

30. Fairlie, Robert W., and Alicia M. Robb. *Race and Entrepreneurial Success: Black-, Asian-, and White-Owned Businesses in the United States.* Cambridge, MA: MIT, 2008. Print.

31. "The Role of Central Banks in Global Macro." *Federal Reserve Economic Review* (2003): 269-314. *Economic Review*. Kansas City Fed, Summer 2003. Web. February 3, 2017. <https://www.kansascityfed.org /Publicat/econrev/Pdf/2q03keet.pdf>, 2nd Quarter

32. Lux, Marshall, and Robert Greene. "The Current State of Banking." *The Future of Banking In a Globalized World* (2012): 1-13. Harvard Kennedy School, February 2015. Web. October 22, 2015; McCord, Roisin, Edward Simpson, and Tim Sablik. *Economic Brief.* Yellowknife: Northwest Territories, Industry, Tourism and Investment, 2007. The Richmond Fed, March 2015. Web. October 22, 2015.

33. Carpenter, John. "Still in Chicago? Peter Thiel Doesn't Think You're 'Very Talented.' Why That's a Problem." *Forbes*. Forbes Magazine, 15 Sept. 2016. Web. December 19, 2016.

34. "Frequently Asked Questions." *YCombinator,* n.d. Web. December 19, 2016. <http://www.ycombinator.com/faq/>

35. Corzine, Nicola. "Venture Capital Isn't the Only Way to Build a 'Successful' Business." *TechCrunch.* N.p., April 21, 2016. Web. December

19, 2016. <https://techcrunch.com/2016/04/21/why-venture-capital -isnt-the-only-way-to-build-a-successful-business/>

36. "The CrunchBase Unicorn Leaderboard." *TechCrunch.* TechCrunch, February 4, 2017. Web. February 6, 2017.

37. Scruggs, Patricia. "The Role of Equity Capital in Rural Communities." *SpringerReference* (2010): 1-79. Mar. 2010. Web. December 21, 2016.

38. Low, Sarah A. "13 Entrepreneurship and Rural Wealth Creation." *Rural Wealth Creation* (2014): 201.

39. Scruggs, Patricia. "The Role of Equity Capital in Rural Communities." *SpringerReference* (2010): 1-79. March 2010. Web. December 21, 2016.

40. "Prospecting." *Lowercase Capital.* Web. December 20, 2016. <https:// lowercasecapital.com/prospecting/>

41. Brush, Candida G., and Patricia G. Greene. "Diana Report Women Entrepreneurs 2014: Bridging the Gender Gap in Venture Capital." *Rep. Arthur M. Blank Center for Entrepreneurship Babson College,* September 2014. Web. December 20, 2016. <http://www.babson.edu /Academics/centers/blank-center/global-research/diana/Documents /diana-project-executive-summary-2014.pdf>

42. Nobel, Carmen. "Venture Investors Prefer Funding Handsome Men." *HBS Working Knowledge.* Harvard Business School, April 30, 2014. Web. December 4, 2015.

43. "Who's the Most Attractive Investment Opportunity of All? Good-looking Men." *Knowledge @ Wharton.* May 26, 2015. Web. March 21, 2017. < http://knowledge.wharton.upenn.edu/article/whos-the-most -attractive-investment-opportunity-of-all-good-looking-men/>

44. Mullainathan, Sendhi, and Marianne Bertrand. "Are Emily and Greg More Employable Than Lakisha and Jamal? A Field Experiment on Labor Market Discrimination." (2004): n. pag. *American Economic Review.* University of Houston, September 2004. Web. December 20, 2016. <http://www.uh.edu/~adkugler/Bertrand&Mullainathan.pdf>

45. Bankoff, Caroline. "How Selling Fax Machines Helped Make Spanx Inventor Sara Blakely a Billionaire." *The Vindicated.* New York Magazine, October 31, 2016. Web. February 6, 2017.

46. Omidyar, Pierre. "How I Did It: eBay's Founder on Innovating the Business Model of Social Change." *Harvard Business Review.* EBay, August 20, 2014. Web. January 3, 2017. <https://hbr.org/2011/09 /ebays-founder-on-innovating-the-business-model-of-social-change>

47. Friedman, Milton. "The Social Responsibility of Business is to Increase its Profits." *The New York Times*, September 13, 1970. Web. March 21, 2017. <http://www.colorado.edu/studentgroups/libertarians/issues /friedman-soc-resp-business.html>

48. Smith, Adam. "Of the Propriety of Action." *Library of Economics and Liberty*. Web. March 21, 2017. <http://www.econlib.org/library/Smith /smMS1.html>

49. Empson, Rip. "YCombinator Backs Its First Non-Profit, Watsi; Paul Graham Says He's 'Never Been So Excited' to Invest." *TechCrunch*. N.p., January 25, 2013. Web. December 20, 2016. <https://techcrunch .com/2013/01/25/y-combinator-backs-its-first-non-profit-watsi-paul -graham-says-hes-never-been-so-excited-to-invest/>

50. Rosenwald, Michael S. "Why Going Green Won't Make You Better or Save You Money." *The Washington Post*. WP Company, July 18, 2010. Web. February 6, 2017. <http://www.washingtonpost.com/wp-dyn /content/article/2010/07/16/AR2010071606839.html>

51. Woodruff, Mandi. "Truck Driving May Be America's Most Popular Job." *Yahoo! News*. Yahoo!, February 6, 2015. Web. February 3, 2017. <http://finance.yahoo.com/news/truck-driving-may-be-america-s -most-popular-job--182859840.html>

52. Altman, Sam. "Moving Forward on Basic Income." *YCombinator*. N.p., January 31, 2017. Web. February 3, 2017. <https://blog.ycombinator .com/moving-forward-on-basic-income/>

53. Trant, Joan E. "Capitalizing on Microfinance: Pursuing Financial Return with Social Impact." (2015): n. pag. Microfinancegateway.org. International Association of Microfinance Investors, 2015. Web. February 3, 2017. <https://www.microfinancegateway.org/sites /default/files/mfg-en-paper-capitalizing-on-microfinance-pursuing -financial-return-with-social-impact-2010.pdf>

54. Microfinance Market Outlook 2016. Rep. *ResponsAbility*, December 2015. Web. December 19, 2016. <http://www.responsability.com /investing/data/docs/en/17813/Microfinance-Outlook-2016-EN.pdf>

55. Grant, Adam M. *Originals: How Non-Conformists Move the World*. New York: Viking, an imprint of Penguin Random House LLC, 2016. Print; Berg, Justin M. "Balancing on the Creative High-Wire." *Administrative Science Quarterly* Volume: 61 Issue: 3, (2016): 433–468. Article First Published Online: March 25, 2016. DOI: 10.1177/0001839216642211.

Johnson Cornell Business., March 25, 2016. Web. February 3, 2017. <http://journals.sagepub.com/doi/abs/10.1177/0001839216642211>

56. Dane, Erik. "Exploring intuition and its role in managerial decision making." *The Academy of Management Review* 32 (1). January 2007.

57. Jain, Pankaj. "Village Capital and the Value of Peer-Based Evaluation." *SOCAP 2011*. Next Billion, September 12, 2011. Web. 3 Feb. 2017. <http://nextbillion.net/socap11-learning-from-village-capital/>

58. Heller, Karen. "The Luxury-Goods Company Shinola Is Capitalizing on Detroit." *The Washington Post*. WP Company, November 17, 2014. Web. February 3, 2017. <https://www.washingtonpost.com/lifestyle /style/the-luxury-goods-company-shinola-is-capitalizing-on-detroit /2014/11/17/638f88a4-6a8f-11e4-b053-65cea7903f2e_story.html ?utm_term=.ebc2ee87995b>

59. Mathews, Rick. "Detroit Bankrupt: To See Detroit's Decline, Look at 40 Years of Federal Policy." *Mic*. N.p., October 25, 2015. Web. December 20, 2016. <http://mic.com/articles/45563/detroit-bankrupt-to-see-detroit -s-decline-look-at-40-years-of-federal-policy>

60. Kelman, Glen. "Why 1 in 4 Silicon Valley Homebuyers Want to Leave." *CNBC*. Redfin, May 21, 2015. Web. January 3, 2017. <http://www.cnbc .com/2015/05/21/soaring-housing-costs-forces-talent-to-flee-silicon -valley.html>

61. "Best breeding ground for unicorns may not be Silicon Valley." *PitchBook*. October 31, 2014. <http://pitchbook.com/news/articles /best-breeding-ground-for-unicorns-may-not-be-silicon-valley>

62. From, Stories, The Field: Eastern Province. "School Leaders Witness Increased Attendance and Enrollment at Schools with Improved Sanitation Infrastructure." (n.d.): n. pag. *WashPlus*. USAID. Web. December 20, 2016. <http://www.washplus.org/sites/default/files /zambia-enrollment2015.pdf>

63. "2016 U.S. TRUST INSIGHTS ON WEALTH AND WORTH." (n.d.): n. pag. *US Trust | Bank of America Corporation*, May 2016. Web. December 20, 2016. 00-21-4307NSB.

64. Baird, Ross. "Bring Your Values to Your Day Job." *The Huffington Post*. TheHuffingtonPost.com, 30 October 2015. Web. February 3, 2017. <http://www.huffingtonpost.com/ross-baird/bring-your-values-to -your-day-job_b_8436072.html>

65. Gurchiek, Kathy. "Millennial's Desire to Do Good Defines Workplace Culture." *Society for Human Resource Management*, July 7, 2014. Web.

December 20, 2016. <http://www.shrm.org/hrdisciplines/diversity /articles/pages/millennial-impact.aspx>

66. Pendlington, David. "Unilever and Its Supply Chain: Embracing Radical Transparency to Implement Sustainability." *S-Lab Final Report* (2010): n. pag. May 12, 2010. Web. February 3, 2017. <http://mitsloan .mit.edu/actionlearning/media/documents/s-lab-projects/Unilever -report.pdf>

67. Saltuk, Yasemin, Amit Bouri, Abhilash Mudaliar, and Min Pease. *Perspectives on Progress, The Impact Investor Survey.* Rep. New York: JP Morgan/ GIIN, 2013. Print.

68. Healy, Beth. "Deval Patrick Takes Investing Role at Bain Capital." BostonGlobe.com. *Boston Globe,* April 14, 2015. Web. February 10, 2017. <https://www.bostonglobe.com/business/2015/04/13/former-gov -deval-patrick-join-bain-capital/QEgS648qXMm2KIq1AUySRO /story.html>

69. Pope Francis. "The Pope's Speech at 'Investing for the Poor 2014'" *Investing for the Poor 2014.* The Vatican. June 2014. Speech.

70. Pendlington, David. "Unilever and Its Supply Chain: Embracing Radical Transparency to Implement Sustainability." *S-Lab Final Report* (2010): n. pag. May 12, 2010. Web. February 3, 2017. <http://mitsloan .mit.edu/actionlearning/media/documents/s-lab-projects/Unilever -report.pdf>

71. "Interview with Tony Carr." Personal interview. 2014.

72. "Interview with Kim Jordan." Personal interview. 2017.

73. Bock, Lazlo. "The Real Reason We Have Unemployment . . . and How to Fix It." *LinkedIn,* October 13, 2014. Web. December 1, 2016. <https:// www.linkedin.com/pulse/20141013220744-24454816-let-s-fix-it -blame-unemployment-on-the-color-blue>

74. "Statistics on U.S. Generosity | The Almanac of American Philanthropy | The Philanthropy Roundtable." Philanthropy Roundtable, 2014. Web. February 3, 2017. <http://www.philanthropyroundtable.org/almanac /statistics/>

75. Smith, Yves. "Can Uber Ever Deliver? Part One—Understanding Uber's Bleak Operating Economics." *Naked Capitalism.* N.p., November 30, 2016. Web. February 3, 2017. <http://www.nakedcapitalism .com/2016/11/can-uber-ever-deliver-part-one-understanding-ubers -bleak-operating-economics.html>

76. Mosher, Eric. "US Private Equity Funds Return 0.2%; US Venture Capital Funds Return -3.3% In 1Q 2016." *Cambridge Associates*. N.p., September 19, 2016. Web. February 1, 2017. <https://www.cambridge associates.com/press-release/us-private-equity-funds-return-0-2-us-venture-capital-funds-return-3-3-in-1q-2016/>

77. Crary, David. "Out of prison, then back in? Unique plan aims to break cycle." *The Associated Press*. May 13, 2017. Web. March 21, 2017. <https://www.apnews.com/19c38842a4dc4c92a08286baeddbc4a6/Out-of-prison,-then-back-in?utm_campaign=SocialFlow&utm_source=Twitter&utm_medium=AP>

78. "What Is a Program-Related Investment?" *GrantSpace*. N.p., 2016. Web. January 3, 2017. <http://grantspace.org/tools/knowledge-base/Grantmakers/pris>

79. Ricker, Thoas. "How Do Tech's Biggest Companies Compare on Diversity?" *The Verge*. N.p., August 20, 2015. Web. February 3, 2017. <http://www.theverge.com/2015/8/20/9179853/tech-diversity-scorecard-apple-google-microsoft-facebook-intel-twitter-amazon>

80. Rock, David and Heidi Grant. "Why Diverse Teams Are Smarter." *Harvard Business Review*, November 4, 2016. <https://hbr.org/2016/11/why-diverse-teams-are-smarter>

81. Crary, David. "Out of prison, then back in? Unique plan aims to break cycle." *The Associated Press*. May 13, 2017. Web. March 21, 2017. <https://www.apnews.com/19c38842a4dc4c92a08286baeddbc4a6/Out-of-prison,-then-back-in?utm_campaign=SocialFlow&utm_source=Twitter&utm_medium=AP>

82. Klein, Freada Kapor, Kimberly Seals Allers, and Martha Mendoza. *Giving Notice: Why the Best and Brightest Leave the Workplace and How You Can Help Them Stay*. San Francisco: Jossey-Bass, 2008. Print.

83. Baird, Ross, and Simon Desjardins. "Show Me What You Can Do." (2015): n. pag. *Shell Foundation*, July 2015. Web. August 4, 2016. <http://www.shellfoundation.org/ShellFoundation.org_new/media/Shell-Foundation-Reports/Show-me-what-you-can-do-Final-low-res.pdf>

84. Walker, Darren. "Internships Are Not a Privilege." *New York Times*. N.p., July 5, 2016. Web. February 13, 2017. <http://m.cn.nytimes.com/opinion/20160705/breaking-a-cycle-that-allows-privilege-to-go-to-privileged/en-us/>. Hunt, Vivian, Dennis Layton, and Sara Prince. "Why Diversity Matters." McKinsey.com. January 2015. Web. April 13,

2017. <http://www.mckinsey.com/business-functions/organization/our-insights/why-diversity-matters>

85. Schulman, Dan. "Teamwork's Rewards." *New York Times*. February 24, 2008. Web, March 21, 2017. <http://www.nytimes.com/2008/02/24/jobs/24boss.html>

86. Schulman, Dan. "Building an Inclusive and Diverse Workforce at PayPal." *PayPal*, August 4, 2016. Web. Dceember 20, 2016. <https://www.paypal.com/stories/us/building-an-inclusive-and-diverse-workforce-at-paypal>

87. Basu, Sandip, David Benson, and Gary Dushnitsky. "Corporate Venture Capital (CVC)." *Kauffman Foundation*. Kauffman Foundation, 2016. Web. February 13, 2017. <http://www.kauffman.org/microsites/state-of-the-field/topics/finance/equity/corporate-venture-capital>.

88. Moore, Daniel. "A Year after Uber Hired Away Researchers, CMU Robotics Center Rebounds." *Pittsburgh Post-Gazette*. N.p., March 7, 2016. Web. December 20, 2016. <http://www.post-gazette.com/business/tech-news/2016/03/07/A-year-after-Uber-hired-away-researchers-CMU-robotics-center-rebounds/stories/201603070110>

89. Long, Judith Grant. *Public/Private Partnerships for Major League Sports Facilities*. Abingdon: Routledge, 2012. Print.

90. Parker, Clifton B. "Sports stadiums do not generate significant local economic growth, Stanford expert says." *Stanford News*, July 30, 2015. Web. March 21, 2017. <http://news.stanford.edu/2015/07/30/stadium-economics-noll-073015/>

91. Corzine, Nicola. "Venture Capital Isn't the Only Way to Build a 'Successful' Business." *TechCrunch*. N.p., April 21, 2016. Web. December 19, 2016. <https://techcrunch.com/2016/04/21/why-venture-capital-isnt-the-only-way-to-build-a-successful-business/>

92. Crain, Nicole V., and W. Mark Crain. "The Impact of Regulatory Costs on Small Firms." *National Association of Manufacturers*, September 10, 2010. Web. January 3, 2017. <http://www.nam.org/Data-and-Reports/Cost-of-Federal-Regulations/Federal-Regulation-Full-Study.pdf>

93. Crain, Mark W., and Crain, Nicole V. "The Cost of Federal Regulation to the U.S. Economy, Manufacturing and Small Business." *National Association of Manufacturers*, September 10, 2014. Web. March 21, 2017. <http://www.nam.org/Data-and-Reports/Cost-of-Federal-Regulations/Federal-Regulation-Full-Study.pdf>

94. Dunkelberg, William, and Holly Wade. *NFIB Small Business Economic Trends*. Nashville: National Federation of Independent Business, 2013. Print.

95. Gardner, Mandy. "SOCAP Voices: Catherine Hoke of Defy Ventures on Transformation, Mass Incarceration, and Entrepreneurship." *Social Capital Markets*, June 21, 2016. <http://socap16.socialcapitalmarkets .net/2016/06/21/socap-voices-catherine-hoke-of-defy-ventures/>

96. Durose, Matthew R., Alexia D. Cooper, and Howard N. Snyder. "Recidivism of Prisoners Released in 30 States in 2005: Patterns from 2005 to 2010." *Bureau of Justice Statistics Special Report*, NCJ 244205 (2014): 31.

97. "Patent Pending: How Immigrants Are Reinventing the American Economy." *The New American Economy*, June 2012. Web. December 20, 2016.<http://www.renewoureconomy.org/wp-content/uploads/2013/07 /patent-pending.pdf>

98. Berman, Jillian, "Class of 2015 has the most student debt in U.S. History." *Marketwatch*, May 9, 2015. Web. March 21, 2017. <http:// www.marketwatch.com/story/class-of-2015-has-the-most-student -debt-in-us-history-2015-05-08>

99. Taylor, Stephen, Brian Oh, and Patrick Macki. "Compensation Policy and Employee Turnover." Factors Affecting Entrepreneurship among Veterans Factors Affecting Entrepreneurship among Veterans (n.d.): 166-82. *Small Business Association*, March 2011. Web. December 20, 2016. <https://www.sba.gov/sites/default/files/files/rs384.pdf>

100. Huffman, Mark. "Why Retailers Are Betting You'll Buy the Extended Warranty." *Consumer Affairs*, July 15, 2016. Web. January 4, 2017. <https://www.consumeraffairs.com/news/why-retailers-are-betting -youll-buy-the-extended-warranty-010715.html>

101. Franklin, Benjamin. *The Autobiography of Ben Franklin*. Sioux Falls, SD: Nu Vision Publications, 2009. Print.

102. Fallows, James. "How America is Putting Itself Back Together Again." *The Atlantic*, March 2016 issue. Web. March 21, 2017. <https://www .theatlantic.com/magazine/archive/2016/03/how-america-is-putting -itself-back-together/426882/>

103. Bishop, Bill. *The Big Sort: Why the Clustering of Like-Minded Americans is Tearing Us Apart*. Boston: Mariner Books, 2009.

104. Bannick, Matt and Goldman, Paula A. "Priming the Pump: The Case for a Sector Based Approach to Impact Investing." *Omidyar Network*,

September 2012. Web. March 21, 2017. <https://www.omidyar.com
/sites/default/files/file_archive/insights/Priming%20the%20Pump
_Omidyar%20Network_Sept_2012.pdf>

105. Helm, Burt. "How Boulder Became America's Startup Capital." *Inc.*,
    December 4, 2013. Web. February 3, 2017. <http://www.inc.com
    /magazine/201312/boulder-colorado-fast-growing-business.html>

106. Feldman, Brian S. "The Decline of Black Business." *Washington
    Monthly*, March/April/May 2017. April 19 2017. <http://washington
    monthly.com/magazine/marchaprilmay-2017/the-decline-of-black
    -business/>

107. Stoller, Matt. "Bigger Corporations Are Making You Poorer." *Vice*, April
    5, 2017. <https://www.vice.com/en_us/article/bigger-corporations
    -are-making-you-poorer>

INDEX

ABOUT THE AUTHOR

© Johnny Shryock Photography

Ross Baird is an entrepreneur and investor who is best known for finding, developing, and investing in entrepreneurs in places and industries where most people aren't looking. He founded Village Capital in 2009 and has worked with hundreds of entrepreneurs in over fifty countries since then. He has visited over a hundred cities worldwide by train, plane, and bus in an effort to find new entrepreneurs and help people supporting them, and he and Village Capital have partnered with over twenty Fortune 500 companies to help large institutions uncover new innovations. Before joining Village Capital, Ross worked for a venture capital firm and was on the founding team of four different startups.

Ross and his work have been featured by more than fifty media outlets, including the *New York Times*, *Bloomberg Business Week*, *Inc.*, and *FastCompany*. He has also lectured in entrepreneurship at the University of Virginia since 2012. He has a MPhil from the University of Oxford, where he was a Marshall Scholar, and a BA from the University of Virginia, where he was a Truman Scholar and a Jefferson Scholar.